A Twentieth Century Bishop

THE BISHOP OF NORWICH IN ROBES FOR THE CORONATION
OF GEORGE VI

A Twentieth Century Bishop

RECOLLECTIONS AND REFLECTIONS

By

BERTRAM POLLOCK, K.C.V.O., D.D.

Late Bishop of Norwich

With a Foreword by

THE HON. HAROLD NICOLSON, C.M.G., M.P.

SKEFFINGTON & SON LTD.

47 PRINCES GATE   ::   LONDON, S.W.7.

Made and Printed in Great Britain at

Greycaines

(Taylor Garnett Evans & Co. Ltd.)
Watford, Herts.

CONTENTS

CHAPTER   PAGE

      INTRODUCTION BY THE HON. HAROLD NICOLSON   .   3

      PREFACE   9

   I.   PARENTAGE AND EARLY YEARS   .   .   .   11

  II.   SCHOOL AND COLLEGE DAYS   .   .   .   16

 III.   MARLBOROUGH AND NEIGHBOURHOOD   .   .   20

 IV.   BISHOP WESTCOTT   25

  V.   ORDINATION   27

 VI.   EDWARD VII   33

 VII.   THE DUKE OF CONNAUGHT   .   .   .   37

VIII.   SIDELIGHTS ON WELLINGTON COLLEGE   .   40

 IX.   ARCHBISHOP BENSON   43

  X.   SCHOOL DISCIPLINE   48

 XI.   PUNISHMENT   52

 XII.   NAVY EXAMINATION   54

XIII.   JULY   57

XIV.   RELIGIOUS TEACHING IN PUBLIC SCHOOLS   .   61

XV.   QUEEN VICTORIA   66

XVI.   FIVE REIGNS   68

XVII.   MY EPISCOPATE   75

XVIII.   A BISHOP'S OFFICE   77

XIX.   DEANS OF NORWICH   80

XX.   THE CORONATION   83

XXI.   SANDRINGHAM   87

XXII.   QUEEN MARY   89

XXIII.   SOME FRIENDS AND ASSOCIATES   .   .   92

XXIV.   LETTERS   96

XXV.   PRAYER   99

XXVI.   BIBLE READING   104

XXVII.   THE REVISED VERSION   .   .   .   109

XXVIII.   CERTAINTY OF FAITH   115

XXIX.   CHURCH AND PEOPLE   120

CHAPTER		PAGE
XXX.	THE NATIONAL ASSEMBLY OF THE CHURCH OF ENGLAND	125
XXXI.	DISESTABLISHMENT	130
XXXII.	HOUSE OF LORDS	137
XXXIII.	SPEECHES	141
XXXIV.	THE LIGHTER SIDE	146
XXXV.	MARRIAGE AND DIVORCE	150
XXXVI.	THE PRAYER BOOK	153
XXXVII.	EDITH CAVELL	157
XXXVIII.	BURIAL AND FACULTIES	159
XXXIX.	BROTHERHOOD	163
XL.	POSTSCRIPT BY MRS. BERTRAM POLLOCK . .	166
	INDEX	173

LIST OF ILLUSTRATIONS

Bertram Pollock in Robes for the Coronation of
George VI . . . . *Frontispiece*

Early Years of Bertram Pollock . . . . *facing page* 28

Bertram Pollock with the Bishop of Durham . . ,, 29

Edward VII at Balmoral . . . . . ,, 60

Bertram Pollock's Consecration, April 8, 1910 . . ,, 61

Group at the Palace on the occasion of the Norwich
Musical Festival, 1924 . . . . . ,, 92

Norwich Cathedral from the Palace Garden, and the
Palace Chapel . . . . ,, 93

Ruin of Gateway to Palace Banqueting Hall . . ,, 93

Queen Mary on her way to laying the Foundation
Stone of St. Catherine's Church, Mile Cross, 1935 ,, 124

The Bishop's Palace from the East . . . ,, 125

The Bishop of Norwich and Mrs. Pollock, 1935 ,, 156

Rosalind Pollock (*right*), daughter of the Bishop of
Norwich, and friend in America, 1941 . . ,, 157

INTRODUCTION

By The Hon. Harold Nicolson

I HAVE BEEN asked to write an introduction to these memoirs. In doing so I wish in the first place to pay a tribute to my old headmaster and to seek, in however slight a manner, to place on record the debt which I owe to him for the sympathy, instruction and encouragement he gave me when a boy. In the second place I am glad indeed to add something to the unduly modest portrait which he has painted of himself.

It must be realized that many of these autobiographical notes were written by Bishop Pollock at a time when he was already failing in health. They were composed, sometimes as a record of past controversies, sometimes as a summary of abiding beliefs, and sometimes merely for the pleasure of recalling the famous people and the interesting characters with whom during his long life he had come into contact. He had little time allowed him in which to reconsider what he had written: still less was he able to prepare his incidental essays for the Press. It may well have been that had he himself been spared to revise the book for publication he would have altered the whole proportion of his memoirs. He might well have felt that certain chapters required more extended treatment whereas others could with advantage be curtailed. It was thought preferable, however, to print his papers more or less as he had left them, to make excisions only where unnecessary repetition was entailed, and not to seek to write for him a book which he himself had been unable to finish.

He had no desire that his memoirs should be read as an expression of his life and character. He agreed with Lord Snell in thinking that "the meaning of life had always seemed immensely more important than its incidents". It is evident at the same time that it was not his intention to compose a theological treatise. "In writing these recollections", he recorded, "it has been my wish, if I could, to prevent them being too heavy. My memories for the most consist of short sketches, not elaborated essays. I have had no desire to publish a solemn volume containing no lighter matter which may raise a smile."

In spite of his natural reticence, in spite of a deep shyness which so many people mistook for pride, the fundamentals of his character do in fact emerge from this book with striking simplicity. Intel-

3

lectually Bertram Pollock was not a simple man. His mind was impatient, rapid, intricate. He possessed a strain of secretiveness which led him to conceal his emotions and his thoughts from all but his closest intimates. Had he adopted a secular career he might well have shown himself to be forceful, ambitious, even worldly. Yet although born with that gift of industrious self-assertion which has raised so many of the Pollock family to eminence, he was also born with a profound vocation for a spiritual life. "I was a lad," he writes, "with a religious disposition, and I never remember a time when I was without the hope of becoming a clergyman." The fascination of his character is based upon this duality. On the one hand the intellectual, the scholar, the man of the world: on the other hand the man of religious vocation, possessed of a faith so deep and so forceful as to submerge all mundane considerations.

What strikes me as strange about these memoirs is that the Dr. Pollock whom I knew so well during the first decade of this century —the great headmaster who raised Wellington College to its present high place among our public schools—seems to be overshadowed by the Bishop of Norwich as well as by the forceful prelate who played so stern and unpopular a part in the Prayer-Book controversy. Having but slight knowledge of Dr. Pollock's episcopate, I am unable to judge whether the proportions which he has given to it in these autobiographical notes are in fact the correct proportions. Yet it seems strange to me that he should have treated with such reticence the great battle which in his early manhood he fought for the sake of Wellington. I am naturally tempted to credit my own affectionate and grateful memories and to consider that, whatever may have been the value of his work at Norwich or in the House of Lords, it was at Wellington College that his remarkable personality found its fullest scope. It is for this reason that I wish in this introduction to furnish some additional clues, to add a special tribute of praise, to Dr. Pollock the headmaster rather than to Dr. Pollock the bishop.

Wellington College was founded as a memorial to the Iron Duke and the original intention of the founders was that it should serve not merely as an orphanage for the sons of officers but in some sort as a military academy. The Prince Consort had devoted to the scheme much of his amazing capacity for detailed planning and there can be little doubt that in his intention the school was to be a counterpart of the many military academies of the Continent. This plan was not welcomed by the other Governors and from the first an attempt was made to render Wellington, not a military orphanage only, but a counterpart of our older public schools. Under Dr. Benson's stern tutelage the college made rapid strides. Dr. Benson was succeeded by Dr. Wickham, a gifted and engaging scholar, who devoted perhaps more time to his edition of *Horace* than to the practical administration of the school. By 1890 the repute, as well as the discipline, of the college had declined; an epidemic of diphtheria disclosed the fact that the whole drainage system was defective and for a space of time the school was transferred to Malvern; but the rumours of insanitary conditions, added to rumours of general laxity, had severely damaged the reputation of the college, and the decline in the prestige of Wellington led to a decline in the number of paying boys entering the school and to a severe crisis in the life of the whole institution.

The Governors of the college decided that a drastic reform was necessary. Under Doctor Wickham's gentle system the school prefects and the captains of games had formed themselves into a sort of prætorian guard, determined to defy the authority of the Master, the house-masters and the assistant masters on every possible occasion. The Governors realized that if disaster were to be averted it would be necessary that Dr. Wickham should be succeeded by a younger man of strong personality capable of establishing his unquestioned authority throughout the school. Their choice fell upon Bertram Pollock, then an assistant master at Marlborough, of only twenty-nine years of age. He went to Wellington in 1893 and left it in 1910. During those seventeen years he completely transformed the school and rendered it one of the most disciplined, if not one of the most enlightened, institutions in the country.

Even in my time the legend persisted that on the last day of his first term at Wellington he summoned the school into the great hall and in their presence publicly caned five of the school prefects who had resisted his authority. Dr. Pollock, when I asked him once whether there was any foundation for this legend, smiled a gentle smile of reminiscent triumph: "No," he said, "the version you have heard is not entirely accurate. There was a conflict of wills: mine won."

By the time I myself reached Wellington there was no question of ill-discipline. The only question was whether the discipline, and the rigid restrictions imposed, were not too severe. There still hung about the college the atmosphere of a military orphanage; the whole system, in its methodical precision, was still suggestive of a cadet school. So convinced were the authorities that Satan was lying in wait for any unoccupied little boy, that some precise occupation was devised for every hour and every minute, whether in the form of compulsory games or in that of compulsory lessons. Nor was this all. The programme was laid down at the beginning of each term and was so rigidly operative that the masters could tell, not only

A*

what any boy was doing at any given moment, but also what the same would be doing at 3.45 p.m. four weeks ahead. This system may well have produced a machine of the very utmost regularity and precision; but it was certainly not good for the mind. I doubt even whether it was good for the character—since it is only by sad processes of trial and error that we learn how to adjust ourselves to our environment. At Wellington College there were no such processes; we seldom, if ever, were allowed freedom of choice; the mechanism worked so perfectly that there was no scope for the organism to develop.

It is against this background, mechanical, rigid and drab, that the humanistic side of Dr. Pollock, and the immense influence he exercised upon those who were closely associated with him, can best be understood. To the smaller boys he appeared as an almost theocratic figure, robed in silk, majestic in appearance, and above all different. Different in the first place from the rather harsh mechanism of the school-system; different in the second place from all the other masters in the school. It may well have been that this sense of difference was deliberately cultivated and exploited; it may have been part of his secret plan. Upon the boys, it had the effect of placing him in a category apart from all the other masters, even from the school itself. However deep the awe with which we regarded him, it was never an impersonal awe. To the other masters he may have seemed aloof and autocratic: I have since realized that he was never very popular with his staff. To us he appeared as something, not so much above everything else, as detached from everything else. Our relation towards him was a direct relation rather than an indirect relation. He was not merely the summit of the whole school, he was also something outside the school, something suggestive of the great exciting world beyond.

As the years passed and we reached the Upper Sixth this feeling of personal relationship expanded quite naturally into close personal contact. So rigid was the school discipline, so mechanical had become our every thought and action, that Dr. Pollock could afford to deal with the older boys in wholly unconventional ways. In place of the ordinary class-room we would sprawl in his garden or gather round the fire in his study. He enjoyed the amenities of civilized life and would provide us lavishly with excellent coffee and little cakes. He was something more than a great scholar; I sometimes wonder even whether his classical scholarship was of the highest order and I suspect that, strangely enough, he almost disliked Greek; but he had a wide knowledge and reverence for classical literature and was able to convey to his chosen pupils the excitement, in place of the drudgery, of learning.

His mind was most attuned to the Latin poets, and he would read with us, in his lovely rapid voice, the greatest passages from the whole of Latin literature.

His method of teaching Latin was wholly personal. When one entered the Upper Sixth he would present one with a little printed card containing what to his mind were the five or six most beautiful lines in the Latin languages. Of these the one he himself most preferred was the startling line of Persius: *"Virtutem videant intabescantque relictâ."* Often and often would he murmur that line, sighing to himself, sighing sometimes with the words "and all the dreary round of sin". We were made to learn by heart, and to recite at unexpected moments, long passages from the Sixth Æneid. *"Manibus date lilia plenis . . ."* some boy would mumble, only to be interrupted by Dr. Pollock—"But please, my dear Watkin, do not say those lines as if you didn't enjoy them." How carefully would he read to us, how gently would he almost intone, the Sirmio elegy of Catullus, swinging suddenly from the sad Latin words to the lovely song of Tennyson. "Row us out from Desenzano to your Sirmione, row . . ." Even to the dullest among us, stretched on pine needles while the sun set behind the trees, the sound of that gentle voice gave intimations of immortality.

In regard to the more precise needs of classical education, for the practical purposes of examinations, Dr. Pollock adopted a wholly different tone. He never concealed from us either his contempt for the examination system or the fact that examinations had got to be passed. He had an irritated dislike of annotated text-books and would refer with scorn to what he called "the notes". I recall how he snubbed one boy, who treated Virgil as something to be mastered for examination purposes only, by forbidding him to read "the notes" for a period of four weeks. "The time," he said, "which you will thereby gain will be devoted to learning by heart a single line of Virgil and repeating it frequently to yourself. At the end of the four weeks you will explain to me why that line is perhaps the most beautiful hexameter ever written. If your explanation is satisfactory, you can then return to your beloved notes." The line, and I agree with Dr. Pollock, was *"Nudus in ignotâ Palinure jacebis arenâ."*

With an amused smile he would give us certain "tips for exams" and particularly in regard to the writing of Latin verses. He would warn us that only when we could write hexameters as well as Virgil wrote them could we allow ourselves the luxury of a spondaic ending on the analogy of *"magni Jovis incrementum"*. He would say to us "some examiners like 'enim' and some do not; one cannot be sure". He would teach us the several tricks of versification, giving to each

trick a pet name of his own. The device, for instance, of shortening
a long sentence by using a parenthesis was called "a filthy cohort".
"This is an occasion," he would say, "when a filthy cohort would
come in useful." I leave it to the ingenious scholar to identify the
origin of this device. He will find it in *Ovid*.

By these subtle and deliberate means Dr. Pollock taught us, not
merely to deal with the tricks and devices of examinations, but more
importantly to understand that Greek and Latin were not dead languages but the fabric of literature itself. His treatment of boys was
a mixture of awe-inspiring authority and the most original humour.
The jokes that he made continually about our work or about our
companions were quite different from the ordinary master's jokes;
I regret that in his memoirs there are so few instances of his sense of
fun. He derived much placid amusement from the strange antics
of little boys. His anger, we felt, could be like the anger of Jupiter;
I suppose I must have seen him angry during the four years I spent
at Wellington; if so, I retain no memory of such occasions; but the
moments when I saw him amused still sparkle for me as the myriad
waves.

But behind all this, behind the gaiety which he brought to teaching
and to discipline, was his immensely devotional attitude towards life.
It was a shock to realize that a man who appeared to be so mundane,
whose humanism was in many ways so elaborate, possessed in religious
matters the fervent simplicity of an anchorite. However intricate or
diverse might be the pattern of his intellectual or worldly attitudes,
his faith was uniform, unvarying, and simple beyond belief. This
man who ruled our little world with such conscious despotism, who
seemed to us to possess all the graces and the power of this world,
would kneel before his God in utter humility, in utter confidence, in
complete abandonment of self. Even upon those of us who had not
been granted the grace of a religious disposition, the utter truth and
simplicity of Dr. Pollock's faith produced a lasting sense of reverence.
"Virtutem videant . . ." he would have murmured gently. And
assuredly those who had the privilege of watching him at prayer caught
a glimpse of virtue not of this world but of the next.

PREFACE

I HAVE THOUGHT that it might be of interest for me to give some record of my long life and of my very long episcopate, in which I have received much kindness in many quarters, and have taken my part in varied events. I have also had occasion to form my own opinion on questions of the times, ecclesiastical or general, which have come to my notice.

How I came to be a twentieth century Bishop I will explain in the coming pages. Then I shall have something to say about the things which came into my life after I had been nominated to the See of Norwich in 1910. While a chance reader may prefer to glance at the outward record, for me the meaning of my actions and outlook stands first, if I may take to myself the more general words of Lord Snell, "the meaning of life has always seemed to me immensely more important than its incidents".

PREFACE

I HAVE thought that it might be of interest for me to give some
account that does not ...

...

CHAPTER I

Parentage and Early Years

MY FATHER WAS the third son of Sir Frederick Pollock, Senior Wrangler in 1806, Attorney-General in Sir Robert Peel's first and second Administrations, who became Chief Baron of the Court of Exchequer in 1844, retiring from that post twenty years later.

My great-grandfather, of Scottish extraction, who lived in what is now Northumberland Avenue, was saddler to King George III and the Royal Family. They were not, I believe, very good at paying their debts. He married a very able woman to whom we owe the characteristic family face. She worked hard for their sons, who in due time achieved eminence. One of them became a Field-Marshal, another Chief Justice of Bombay, a third enjoys the unknown fame of being the inventor of the circulating stirrup-strap. My father, born in 1821, succeeded his eldest brother—the second Sir Frederick— as the Queen's Remembrancer in 1886. He had a profound respect for this brother, in whose mind and bearing there was a real greatness and rare charm, though he had not the world-fame of his son, the third baronet. His admiration for his father was unbounded, and he would constantly tell stories that concerned my grandfather's days at the bar. My grandfather was at York Assizes. It was his way to work up his briefs very early in the morning. The *Heart of Midlothian* had just been published and he had it by his side in his room, and instead of turning to his brief he began to read it, and went on reading it till it was time to go into Court; but with a fine self-assurance he opened the case. It was a commercial case involving much correspondence, so he informed himself of the rights and wrongs of his client by reading aloud a succession of letters until the Judge interposed and said: "Is it really necessary that we should hear all these letters in detail one by one?" My grandfather's reply was: "I regret, My Lord, that it *is* necessary".

To my grandfather, I believe, is attributed the story of an ingenious argument. Doubtful as to the value, in many instances, of quoting cases, he undertook to refer to any case, however far-fetched, mentioned to him by his friends, in the next case he was to conduct. He did this— and the Judge made a note of it.

I believe that at times he did not rely much upon the evidence of handwriting experts. If this was so, it may have been because he could imitate perfectly himself the handwriting of other people. He would ask a man to dinner in the man's own handwriting. I have a letter in front of me in which he imitated quite exactly the writing of each of us when as children we sent him good wishes, signing our own names.

There was a constellation of brilliant speakers practising on the Northern circuit, and one day my father or a friend of his heard—at York—some yeoman farmers and people of that class estimating and comparing the various great men. At the end of the conversation someone said: "But what about Scarlett?" (created Lord Abinger in 1835), whose name had not so far been mentioned. The reply was given: "We don't think much of him—he is so lucky, he is always on the right side."

Can one think of a more perfect testimony offered to the skill of an advocate?

As a lad my father would sometimes go down to the House of Commons with my grandfather. One night he fell asleep. The police found him and took him for a sort of Guy Fawkes. Fortunately, as he was being led off under arrest to the Clock Tower, he saw a member he knew leaving the House late and shouted after him. His friend turned back and vouched for his identity and character.

Though the Law gave him his profession, my father had an acquaintance with all kinds of things outside the Law, and readily made friends with those who were concerned in them. In his later years he interested himself in the early developments of photography, and on his death-bed, when he was ninety-three, he was making plans concerning submarines.

One day he had missed his train and, finding a single engine soon afterwards passing slowly through the station, jumped on to it. He received a cold welcome at first, but knew so much about it all that when it was pulled up at a signal, the driver, now his friend, gave him hints how best to proceed on his journey. He rode every successive type of bicycle. If a workman came to the house for any purpose, my father at once got alongside of him. A limit, however, to his singular gift of friendship was shown when, in seeking a small club near Waterloo Station—where his train started—and finding, as he thought, just what he wanted, he was put off on hearing from the manager that he hoped he realized he would chiefly meet betting men there.

My brother, acquainted with my father's friendly ways, once found himself mistaken. They were visiting Greenwich on the Grand Day and my father was soon in conversation with an old man who looked anything but smart, and my brother wished that they might take notice of some of the many distinguished people who were going the rounds. As they passed a certain statue the old gentleman stood side-by-side with it and said: "What do you think of that?" It was easy to see that it represented this aged man when he was in his prime. It was Sir George Airy, formerly Astronomer-Royal for forty-six years.

My father was the intimate friend of the John Murray of his day, who gave him Darwin's *Origin of Species* to read through, and on the strength of my father's advice doubled the first edition, though this book did not bring to the firm the outstanding and continuous success of *Little Arthur's History of England*.

He was much interested in mechanical subjects and I remember as a boy finding his explanations of them tedious to follow; mechanics have never appealed to me. He delighted in his telescope and he had a considerable knowledge of physiology; when, as a child, in climbing a tree, I fell and had a severe cut on my face, he ingeniously treated it without any stitches. His grasp of many other subjects, like organ building, etc., was remarkable. He knew much about birds and flowers. He went thoroughly into any subject that at the moment interested him, and would get to the bottom of it; for example, nautical almanacks disproved for him the 'struggling moonbeam's misty light' at the burial of Sir John Moore after Corunna. When as a boy he had mislaid something, one of his brothers remarked: "Have you looked for it in the cyclopædia, which you are always searching?" He was a man very much beloved and he had a warm sympathy with the interests of others.

There was no self-advertisement about him; nothing petty or small in his outlook, which was objective rather than philosophical. He had a great knowledge of human nature and made allowances accordingly. It was from my father that I received my earliest lessons in Latin and Greek—when he was shaving and dressing—and I can now remember the first Latin verse I wrote before I went to school. By precept and example my father directed me to talk of things and not of people, in the sense of trivial gossip which leads the way to disparagement and unfriendly criticism. Wise observations of his remain with me, such as: "If you want to please people you must please them in their own way." "A gentleman must be able to hide his feelings."

My mother was the eldest daughter of the Reverend Henry Herbert, Rector of Rathdowney, Queen's County. She belonged to a distinguished Irish family, and my father's father described her as "one of the human or (as far as I know) angelic beings: I don't believe any angel is better". She was a remarkable needlewoman of those days; she shared with my father his gift for friendship. Her warm Irish heart went out to others in a delightful way; she was always anxious that anyone who came to the house should take something away—flowers, fruit, etc. With her I read my Bible—her religious shelves were full—and I used to attend her working parties. I remember well her beautiful singing in church. She thought it better for me not to look at the *Illustrated London News* pictures of the Franco-Prussian War, when Strasbourg, Metz, and Marshal Bazaine were familiar names to me.

I was the youngest of my family, with four surviving brothers and two sisters. It would be difficult to over-estimate what I owed in my childhood, boyhood, and later years to my father and mother, and to my brothers and sisters.

My sister Haddie (senior by ten years) and I have always been the greatest friends. Even in her old age and weak health, by her sympathy and understanding, she wins the hearts of those whom she meets; there is an unmistakable quality in her company and her voice, appreciated by all but the wholly self-centred.

In my childhood I owed much to my nurse, Elizabeth King. She was a friend of Jenny Lind, the superb singer, who lived near our first home in Wimbledon. Jenny Lind was naturally sensitive lest her talent should be exploited for private entertainment. Asked one evening to sing, after a dinner-party, she refused. The hostess then turned to my mother, who complied at once. This kind act, which saved an awkward situation, so much impressed Jenny Lind, that she immediately changed her mind and sang herself.

My nurse, 'Lizzy', as we called her, was a devoted friend of the family, and there were certain principles in her mind which her consistent example impressed on me. I have often been able to trace back to her influence ideas and habits for which, as time has gone on, I have found my own good reasons. For example, there was her love of the Bible, her honesty and dread of debt, her respect for Sunday, Sunday worship, and Sunday school, her devoted industry, her just estimates. She taught me that even worse than making an unkind remark was to repeat one. I was, perhaps, as the youngest of the family, thrown with her more than my brothers and sisters, who had older friends or were away at school.

My first appearance in public life was when the new Lord Mayor came, as was usual, into the old Court of Exchequer, which then sat at Westminster, to be received by the Lord Chief Baron and the Barons of the Exchequer. Being a very little boy I was allowed to sit on the Bench with the Judges. An uncle of mine lived to be the last of these Barons, whom the Judicature Act of seventy years ago discontinued. To the delight of my nurse and others, the newspapers next day related the incident and described me as 'a pretty little boy with turn-down collar and shining morning face'.

I have some vivid recollections of my childhood. I remember riding on a donkey into the neighbouring village and being thrown off and breaking my arm. I was carried into a grocer's shop close by. A saw for cutting bacon bones was brought in to make the splints the right size for binding up my little arm. When I viewed the saw I felt that I was exceeding any rights I had in the matter by saying that I would prefer to keep my arm on if they didn't mind. I was six years old and I used from time to time to visit a cousin of my father's, a surgeon in London, for the breakage was a serious one and my elbow has never been quite right. Everyone was most kind to me, helping me in and out of buses—the horse-drawn vehicles of that time. With the self-centredness of a child I could not think what had happened when, in the end, the sling was taken off and no one helped me any longer.

We lived a quiet life in the country, and we used to fish in a stream close by and I announced one day that I was going to catch a bloater. I was fond of bird-nesting by myself and I cultivated a life-long love of birds. Occasionally we had a day in London, and one day we went to lunch with an uncle who was going to take us to the Zoo. It was a badly arranged meal, for I found myself drinking a wine-glassful of audit ale before I had eaten anything. This proved too much for me, and when we got into Regent's Park I went and struck a policeman, being able to reach his legs—no higher. On this my brothers held me firmly by the hand. It is possible that this unfortunate lapse of mine in these early days helped towards my taking the total abstinence pledge when I was a boy at school, a pledge to which I have always adhered.

My brother Ernest, better known to the world as Lord Hanworth, the Master of the Rolls, and I were called 'the little boys'. I was rightly overshadowed by him, for he was an engaging small boy and even in those early days showed that striking gift of companionship which throughout his career won the affection of a large and growing circle. If anyone came to see us it was he, not I, who did the talking. In many ways I was silent and solitary in my demeanour and disposition. I was privileged to enjoy a singularly happy, united, and devout home; for which, when I was growing up, I used to thank God, for I was a lad with a religious disposition, and I never remember a time when I was without the hope of becoming a clergyman.

CHAPTER II

School and College Days

MY FIRST SCHOOL was at Eagle House, Wimbledon, and I can to this day recall the clank of its iron gate, which I heard as a homesick child. My godmother, Miss Peache, who lived close by, would come and visit me there. She was generous to me as to many others. She was a friend of my mother and used annually to come and stay with us for a week in the spring. She played croquet when it was a simple game, and we saw to it that she should win. With her wealthy brother she built St. John's Hall, Highbury, for the training of clergy.

The Vicar of Wimbledon once preached a sermon in which he said he was well content with the liberality of the well-to-do members of his congregation, but he eagerly wished that those who were not so well off would give more. He wanted to see more small silver coins in the collection: in those days it was rare for worshippers to give pence. Miss Peache, who was organist, used to walk home with him. The next Sunday he kept her waiting a long time. When he joined her, he said that he seldom received so quick a response to a sermon. He had never seen so many threepenny-bits in a collection. He was crestfallen when Miss Peache remarked: "I put in five pounds' worth of them."

At my preparatory school I began my running activities (which ended in my representing Cambridge as the second string for the quarter-mile against Oxford) in a very humble way: every word describing my prize marks a step down, for I carried off the third prize for the junior consolation handicap.

When I was twelve I moved on to Charterhouse. The school had —by the genius and patient exertions of the resourceful headmaster— recently been transferred from London; the old pensioners of the type of Colonel Newcome continuing in their old quarters. I went up the school rather fast, being usually first in my class, and it would have been better for me if I had had rather more supervision and advice in my general reading, and had been encouraged to study history, ancient and modern, in the interesting way in which the history of England and other countries is now put before boys; and if I had received some useful guidance in choosing and reading the English Classics. I worked easily and I had plenty of time to spare.

I suppose it would be to put myself out of my generation if I expressed any regret for the way in which we would read *Thucydides*, even the magnificent sixth book, without having the background interestingly explained, and as if the bald translation of the Greek was all that mattered. We missed any conception of his philosophy of life, and the insight which makes him the contemporary of every generation.

I had an affectionate admiration for Dr. Haig-Brown, the Headmaster, in whose house I was. There are drawbacks to the plan of a Headmaster having a 'house', and there is a greater independence of position when he can devote himself to his work of teaching and administration of the whole school, and no set of boys has a special claim on his attention. However, I was most fortunately placed, and found the best of friends in my own Headmaster.

At the end of my school career I reached a position of leadership as the Head of the House, where I occupied the bed in which Thackeray, himself a Carthusian, died. There can be no doubt that the senior boys in a great school enjoy excellent opportunities and become fitted for public service in the wider world if their sympathies are not too far concentrated on the old school. But this kind of training only falls to the boys at the top, and is not the necessary privilege of the whole number. The younger boys, however, do have the advantage of belonging to a well-ordered community.

I could read at home as well as at school, and my brothers thought at this time that my taste for sport was not what it should be. So one day they sent me off with a gun to Hounslow Heath—a very different place from what it is now. I took with me a book on the Greek Poets which engrossed my attention so fully that I sat quite still as I read it. The rabbits which abounded there ignored me. When it was time to go home I took a steady aim at a sitting rabbit, fired my gun and killed it. When I went to pick it up I saw that I had killed a second rabbit seated behind the first. One shot, two rabbits! My brothers were silent, if not yet convinced that I was a sportsman.

I fell at Charterhouse under the spell of that beautiful scholar, T. E. Page, a life-long friend to me. He was a great authority on Horace, and famous at Cambridge for his power in Latin versification. He wrote a pretty epigram upon a portrait of Dr. Haig-Brown, to whom the school owed an immense debt in all that his removal of it to the delightful hill near Godalming involved. Page was dissatisfied with the picture as lacking in life and vigour:

> *En faciem! Mentem pictor catus abdidit: illam*
> *Tota tibi ostendit Carthusiane domus.*

(Here is your portrait, the artist has cleverly concealed your mind. But Charterhouse itself is its manifestation.)

Latin verses are now decried as a part of a classical curriculum at school. This may be right when there are so many competing subjects. But apart from their charm, they used to help boys towards that important capacity for later life, of remembering in due proportion many things at once. I used to notice that a boy, with his mind fixed upon the metre, would make blunders of grammar, etc., which he would have avoided in prose composition. It was a remarkable thing for me that, when I went to Trinity, I was under A. W. Verrall a very learned, ingenious, arresting, and persuasive scholar, to whom I am very specially indebted for what he taught me and for what he was to me. No two men could have been more dissimilar in their approach to the classics than Page and Verrall. Each by his own method had climbed to the very highest that Cambridge could offer. It was an illumination to be allowed to share the minds of both.

Verrall often came to Wellington and stayed with me in order to examine the senior boys. Of course he did this excellently and had some stories to tell of adventures in such work. At one school the candidates were so placed in the hall that some boys were writing Greek Prose, others French translation. There was some confusion in the collection of the papers. Missing two of the Greek Prose papers, for which he was responsible, he sent to ask if the French examiner had them. He had; and he sent them across already marked.

My college was Trinity—the family college, I might call it. There were nine members of my family 'up' at the same time, though not all at Trinity. We all went together to a dance at one of the Ladies' colleges, and our names were announced one after another.

After lodging in Rose Crescent for my first term I went into college, and my rooms were at B Great Court on the ground floor. I had two bed-makers in succession to look after me, to wash up and do the rooms and make my bed. We became friends. One of them had a gloomy assistant whose husband deserted her. When the bed-maker told me about it she said, by way of defending the man: "Well, Mrs Plum, I sez to her, I wonder he did not do it long ago; you're *that* dull." She gave me her photograph. This led my cousin to ask his bed-maker for hers. She explained to him she had not got a photograph of herself, but would be glad to give him one of her father when he was a little boy.

The extensive top floor was occupied by H. A. J. Munro, the famous scholar, who led the way as an interpreter and editor of *Lucretius*. My reading was directed to the classical tripos for the first three years; but I also attended divinity lectures. In my fourth year I began to take up Hebrew. I worked hard but did not sit up late for reading. I was found at leisure when many men were beginning their day's or night's work. An early riser, I was regular at morning chapel, which then held a more definite place in college life. Running provided my athletic outlet, and I was often on the track at Fenners and made many running friends. I never 'went into training' by eating or avoiding special foods, and the hours I kept, themselves made a kind of training. I was never a smoker. Domestic arrangements were much less comfortable than they are now in college. I had no access to any bathroom. As a new-comer I had to dine at the first dinner of the three served every day in the College Hall at about 4.0 or 5.0; there was one aged don who, by his own choice or habit, did this daily.

College life for the dons was beginning to change. The marriage of many of them, which was now permitted by a change in University regulations, reduced their attendance in hall, for they now dined in their own homes. About twenty brides came into Cambridge after my first or second long vac. The dons also saw less of one another in their afternoon 'grinds'.

I was a member of the Church Society and became its President, inviting many distinguished men to address it. I had close associations with Addenbrooke's Hospital where my elder brother, Rivers, was appointed House Surgeon. He 'came up' after me, and was a remarkable hurdler, in fact in the 'Varsity sports against Oxford he won the hurdles in what was then the record time. This led to a very severe illness, through which he was most skilfully and tenderly nursed in the hospital: everyone seemed to have overheard the ill-considered remark of one of his early medical teachers—"Remember that *private patients* do not like pain". All this gave me, in my constant visits to him, the chance of coming to know the distinguished medical staff of the hospital—Professor Humphrey, Sir George Paget, and so on. I have kept up my friendship with Miss Paget, who married Sir J. J. Thomson, O.M., Master of Trinity. They have welcomed me to Trinity Lodge in recent years.

I took my degree with a first-class in the Classical Tripos in 1882. In the same class list were found the names of three other future bishops, Kempthorne of Lichfield, Donaldson of Salisbury, and Frere of Truro. We heard our names read out in the Senate House, unlike my grandfather who had to go and look at the list, in which his name appeared, pinned to the door of the Senate House. (He read it downwards, and when he reached the name of Bolland (who also became a Judge) he remarked to himself: "I *must* have beaten Bolland." So he read the list again, and found that his own name stood first, but the pin attaching the list to the door had concealed it.)

In 1903, several years before I became a Bishop, I took the final degree of D.D. For the latter I had to submit a printed volume. The B.D. degree I had taken shortly before, by a method now abandoned. I wrote an essay in Latin and it was to be read before the Regius Professor of Divinity, Dr. Swete, the kindest of friends, in the presence of the University. After the essay had been read, it was his part to refute the candidate in an argument on the subject: the whole exercise to take one hour. It seemed to me that if I wrote an essay which it would take an hour to read, there would be no time left for the refutation. I found that the presence of the University was represented by the door of Dr. Swete's private room in the Divinity School, where the examination took place, being left ajar for the first few minutes. When I had been reading for half an hour, the Professor said: "Shall we take the rest as read?" My little plan was therefore upset, but we had an interesting talk in English. And I ought to add that while I was enjoying Dr. Swete's hospitality the night before, he had already told me that he approved of my exercise. I took the B.D. degree on the same day that I had read to him the first half of my exercise. A few months afterwards my brother Rivers and I took our doctor's degree on the same day: he became M.D.; I, D.D. And there was a paragraph in *The Sportsman* on the double event of two 'Blues' who were brothers proceeding to the degree of doctor in the Senate House at the same time. Later on my other brother, Ernest, later Master of the Rolls, received the honorary degree of LL.D. He was Deputy High Steward of the University.

CHAPTER III

Marlborough and Neighbourhood

WHEN I WENT as one of the Sixth Form masters to Marlborough and made my professional start in the world, I was rather at sea, knowing nothing of the school or the place, but I soon made friendships among the boys, some lasting to the present day, and I became much attached to the neighbourhood. I have never outgrown my affection for the rolling Wiltshire Downs and the town, which lies in a dip in them; standing at a high altitude, one could easily in a walk reach nine hundred feet above sea level. With a sense of loneliness in my heart I would often walk among the beauties of Savernake Forest close by.

I did not then know any members of the Aylesbury family—it was in later years that the present Marquess became my friend. There was a rapid succession of holders of the title; the Marchioness Marie—who in previous years had been well known to the Headmaster of the time—was a famous figure in Victorian days. (It is said of her that when the Court was at Osborne she was staying in the Isle of Wight and on a Sunday went to church at Whippingham. When she arrived with her friend they found the church already crowded out. She remarked in a very audible voice: "We cannot stay here, there is no room"—it was in the days of crinoline—"but anyhow, my dear, we have done the civil thing".)

I had not much time for roaming about, for I found the work exacting. There were the hours spent in class, and many exercises to be corrected and returned to the boys individually; also there was then a system of private tuition, and the boys who wished to have it from any of the Masters would come in a group, out of school hours, to the Masters' rooms. After a few years I became quicker.

To begin with, my inexperience was against me; and whereas, when I was myself the pupil I would instinctively avoid doubtful ways of expression, it was necessary to form a judgment when these were served up in the boys' Greek and Latin compositions. It is also a temptation to a teacher, young or old, to teach too much at once. A boy can only digest a certain portion at a time, and it helps him more if he tries to grasp firmly a certain amount, with the exceptions and irregularities left over for the moment.[1] Many preachers only confuse the minds of their hearers if their words lose in directness of appeal through an unsuccessful comprehensiveness.

I learnt much from colleagues in the common room, where the unmarried Masters took their meals. One would hear casually, in quite an informal but suggestive way, of what had happened in another Master's sphere and how he had dealt with some little perplexity. Many of the boys with whom I was thrown were sons of the clergy; they had been brought up among books, and, so to speak, respected them. This had two advantages: a university course seemed to them the natural sequel of their school days; but if they were to proceed to it, they must win scholarships for themselves, their fathers not being sufficiently well off to send them to Oxford or Cambridge without assistance. The presence of such boys in the school affected its general tone. To encourage them in their own reading I used to provide on some afternoons a tea-party on a large scale, but it was a tea-party for work and not for social conversation.

[1] Canon Bradley has reminded us that to know what to omit is the mark of the true teacher.

The school had not been very successful in its inception. In fact there had been a famous 'rebellion' of the boys in its early years. But Cotton, afterwards Bishop in India, Bradley, eventually Dean of Westminster, and Farrar had consolidated its prestige. It was while Farrar was Head Master that he wrote his *Life of Christ*, which had a great reputation and is still a book, careful, reverent and readable, not to be ignored. His published school sermons illustrate his immense fund of quotations. G. C. Bell was the Master under whom I served: he showed me much personal kindness.

My subjects were Greek and Latin. In teaching I often found that after a boy had gone on much the same in his efforts for a long time, a sudden or complete illumination would dawn on his whole work, especially when the boys who were in front of him were removed. The change was really in him and not in my own observation of him when he had come into a more prominent position.

Another thing worth remembering in all the relations of life, public, personal, and domestic, which teaching made very plain, was the power of praise as compared with blame. A boy praised for some good point in his exercise would remember it, and add that little praiseworthy item to his stock-in-trade. Blame never inspired, and it might provoke hopelessness or resentment. There is nothing like teaching him to reveal the mind and disposition of the pupil at any time of his life: the teacher and the taught get very near together. Perhaps we provided too much Greek and Latin, but the boys I taught had reached the stage of literary appreciation and could follow the niceties and neatnesses of expression. Most boys never got further than the elementary drill, much the same in either language. We are apt to forget how much of the substance of Classical Authors can be acquired from the many excellent translations within reach to-day. It is not the same thing as reading the original, though giving a good general background.

It must be borne in mind that besides the substance of the author, one who is set to read an ancient writer obtains a training in judgment and argument. The whole approach to the point is frequently different in ancient and modern thought: the meaning is expressed in an unfamiliar style. It is often a matter of consideration and opinion which of several interpretations admissible in rendering a phrase is the correct one. But one must not concentrate on the difficult and arguable passages so exclusively as to pay little attention to what is easier and often more arresting and beautiful.

It was while I was at Marlborough that I was ordained; of this more later. The fine school chapel was consecrated in my first term.

For military and other reasons, and owing to the arrival of the motor-car, there are now more people moving about in this area of England, as elsewhere, than was the case in the days of which I am writing. One can still enjoy the majestic sweep of the downs, and Marlborough is not far from Silbury Hill—which the Roman road had to skirt—or from Avebury with its Saxon church and great stones. It was usual for one or other of my colleagues to join the large party which crowds to Stonehenge for the dawn of the longest day, when the sun rises behind the votive stone. My first visit there was in mid-winter, as it happened, before in any way its surroundings were opened up, and then indeed it was impressive—not to say solemn—in its loneliness. All the way to Devizes, 'The Vize' as the country folk would call it, this unenclosed country prevails.

I remember once going over to the Assizes in the little county town, where in the market-place is recorded the fate of Ruth Pierce in 1753. She had protested that she had given her share towards a joint payment for a sack of wheat, "she wished she might drop down dead if she had not", and this very fate overtook her with the money in her hand.

My uncle was the Judge of Assize when I paid my visit: he was trying a murder case. The prisoner was found guilty, and I shall always remember the manner in which the sentence of death was passed and the Baron urged the poor fellow to use the intervening time in seeking "the pardon never refused to the repentant sinner". I remember, too, the wisdom of the Judge who in an interval asked his Marshal (who was his son) to read an important letter he had just written so that his son might learn the kind of letter that is sent by a capable man in public life. It was a bit of education for a young man.

I have, as a Bishop, two or three times visited or written to a man under sentence for murder. One I visited in the gaol at Ipswich. I wished to make sure of his frame of mind before confirming him. He had a very good fellow as his warder, when I went into the condemned cell, who had been reading to him from the Bible. I asked him what had recalled him to his better self. He told me that in the hospital where he was treated, for he had tried to kill himself too, the nurse had said something that helped him: I have frequently mentioned this to encourage nurses, who are often in doubt whether to speak or keep silence. He also told me that what he had learnt in Sunday school as a child came back to him: this I have recounted to Sunday school teachers. By this time he had reassured me. Another man in Norwich did, also, and on the morning of his execution he wrote to me a very beautiful letter.

Before I went to Marlborough, just after taking my degree, I myself travelled as Judge's Marshal on the Western circuit. The Marshal's duty of swearing in the grand jury has now disappeared. Field J. was my Judge; later, he was joined by Hawkins, from whom I learnt two things. Judges had by that time to make notes of a case as it went along. He did so. But when the time came for him to sum up, he closed his book and handed it to his clerk. Taking a scent bottle in his hand, he would speak easily and directly to the jury, without any disconcerting interruption of looking into his notebook for dates or other items. The other thing I remember was the strict chronological order he kept in telling the story. He did not, like Dickens, pursue one part of his narrative at a time independently of the rest, but all that happened on any date he recounted as belonging to the date. He said that once or twice in a big trial he had spoken as counsel or judge for days and days without consulting a note.

I did not play games with the boys at Marlborough but I used to umpire at their athletic sports, and I remember one day coming in from the sports to find a telegram in my room saying that I had been elected Master of Wellington College. I had previously, of course, appeared before the Committee of Selection, consisting of Sir P. Talbot in the chair, Archbishop Benson, Sir Lintorn Simmons, Henry Duke of Wellington, and others. The Master of Trinity was there, and when invited to speak said: "May I first, Mr. Pollock, ask if I am correct in thinking that Mr. Horton Smith is an old pupil of yours?" When I replied that this was so, he added: "Let me then congratulate you; for we have to-day awarded to him the Porson Prize"—that is the great University prize for Greek verse. This was rather telling! My election was later confirmed at Marlborough House by the Prince of Wales, the Chairman, and the whole body of Governors. I may add that in this sense the Prince of Wales sent me to Wellington, just as, sixteen years later, it was he, when he was King, who sent me (then as now not very intimate in professional ecclesiastical circles) to Norwich. To him I did my homage three days before his death.

CHAPTER IV

Bishop Westcott

IN THOSE DAYS Bishop Wordsworth (one of the great Wordsworth family) was the Bishop of Salisbury. He was the son of Bishop Wordsworth of Lincoln. The Lincoln Bishop was a very earnest man, and again and again he looked back to the history of the early church for guidance which should help him in his own work. He sometimes attributed to other people a knowledge they did not possess. He was arguing some point before the rustic churchwardens of Lincolnshire and suddenly stopped and said: "I know what you are thinking. You are saying to yourselves: 'In all this has not the Bishop forgotten the second council at Ephesus?'" of which, of course, they had never heard, but he wove it into his argument. John Sarum was no less learned and he must have developed early, for it is told of him that when he was a little child, not yet able to speak, on seeing the nursemaid helping herself to jam from the cupboard he said to himself: "I shall report that when I can speak." He was a great ally of Archbishop Benson, and when the Archbishop begged him to do a certain piece of work for him he wrote back, saying, "I fear I have not the time; it would take me an hour a day, and, as it is, I only have six hours for my night's rest." Benson's rejoinder was, "Let me warn you against self-indulgence: all through my life I have found a five hours' night quite enough. Follow my example and you will exactly save the one hour you speak of."

The Bishop of Salisbury allowed me to accept the invitation of Bishop Westcott (who had just gone to Auckland Castle to open his episcopate of Durham), and I was to read with him. So far as this related to the passing of an examination this plan did not come to very much; when I approached him with some little difficulty he would characteristically lift my mind from the small point at issue and reveal to me the greater and eternal background with which it was related. That was his way, and his teaching has stayed with me all my life. When he was appointed to that famous Bishopric many who were acquainted with his reputation as a scholar said that he was no man to administer a great industrial diocese. But they changed their minds when he took a leading part in the settlement of a grave and crucial dispute between owners and workers in the mining industry. Perhaps the best-known of Bishop Westcott's labours as a scholar was the joint work that he did with Professor Hort in clarifying the text of the New Testament. It was a monumental task and it still stands with little modification, except that it is now considered that what they called the Western Text was less homogeneous than they had supposed. His magnificent commentary on St. John is a masterpiece and no one can attempt to edit the gospel again without constant reference to it.

One often learnt from him when people came to lunch and one listened to his replies to some of their questions following the consistency of his reasoning. He had some rather special views about the shooting of game in large quantities: "If those are your views," said his guest, "you ought never to eat game." "I never do," was the rejoinder. Someone was arguing about playing games, and the Bishop maintained that the aim of a game should be not to win a personal victory, but to press the team work of the players. But you could not have a game in which you did not wish to win! "I thought you could"—such a phrase was always a sign of difficulty coming. "Then do please mention one such game." "Battledore and shuttlecock," was the Bishop's answer.

A good lady once complained to him that she thought the phrase in the Holy Communion about the burden of our sins being intolerable was exaggerated, and he gave the reply: "Can you walk along a London street on a Saturday night and not say 'the burden of our sins is intolerable'." "Ah, but I was thinking of *myself* and *my* sins." "If you come to the Holy Communion to think of yourself you miss its meaning."

He would refer to the exact words of Apostolic teaching, never presuming beyond the warrant of Scripture, hesitating to make any definition or draw any line that would limit heavenly truth. To him theology was poetry. He was averse from the ways of those who look upon Christian doctrine as comprised in some stereotyped formula reiterated from the past, or draw sharp lines to obtain precision of dogma, and he would say that they omitted whole realms of truth which were on the other side of the line. The Incarnation offered an interpretation for every need and situation in the life of man as they arose from age to age.

He viewed Holy Scripture as no dead record from the past, but luminous as a present gospel for present needs. He was far more anxious to learn the truth that an opponent possessed than to triumph over his errors. He rejoiced to welcome the truths of modern science, especially that of the unity and solidarity of Nature and life, finding in that the counterpart of St. Paul's teaching on the unity of all things in Christ. The Bishop was no socialist, teaching that all men are equal; he was a socialist who taught that the idea of life was that each

n his own place should serve the whole. "Nothing in this world is
our own except our opportunities, and over these is written 'Occupy
till I come.' Sacrifice alone is fruitful." The power of his teaching
has recently reasserted itself and come back into its own. It is
behind much of the thought and many of the ideas of our own time
and the social implications of the New Testament as they are now
seen. But his own attitude to the complex questions of our generation
in peace or war will have been misapprehended by those who think
that they can be solved through earthly systems, unrenewed by a
constant reference to the eternal order.

He loved simplicity of life and was delighted when we left the huge
castle and went for a stay at a seaside cottage near Whitby. I sat
and did my work in a cabbage garden. He and his papers occupied
the little sitting-room at the back of the village shop and he remarked:
'I have not had such a good morning's work since I left Cambridge."

He believed in the value of routine work. No doubt much of a
Bishop's work needs no special gifts for its accomplishment, if he is
industrious and regular and careful. Bishop Westcott rightly felt
that such routine steadies the judgment and offers a firm foothold
from which to soar to the higher flights of thought, scholarship and
enterprise.

His face was marked by deep lines of thought and his grey eyes
constantly seemed to be looking into the beyond. But no one who
ever saw it could forget the beauty with which his smile suffused
his countenance, and lit it up with the beams of radiant glory.

His wife died a short time before he did. Many an aged man
in such bereavement would have spoken of his dreary loneliness, and
have felt brave if he had expressed a hope that he might bear up so
long as need be, in the hope of meeting again in the world to come.
But what did he say? Just this: "And now the memory of a beautiful
life is complete and changeless, a light for the days to come."

CHAPTER V

Ordination

HAVING SPOKEN OF my Ordination and of the incalculable debt which
I owe to the great Bishop of Durham in that connection and ever
afterwards, I now have something to say about the manner of my

own Ordination at Salisbury, and of the way in which I myself con
ducted Ordinations at Norwich and also of the Ordination of school
masters. Bishop Westcott used to say to me: "My heart is still wit
the schoolmasters. Theirs is the most truly pastoral work."

In the winter of 1941 I reached the Jubilee of my ordination t
the Priesthood. I was ordained at Salisbury only a year or tw
before leaving Marlborough. Ever since a child it had been m
unwavering hope and intention to be ordained, and I should not hav
contemplated a schoolmaster's career without ordination.

For an assistant master, ordination adds a new savour to h
work, and not only as regards preaching sermons or preparing boy
for confirmation. It brings his teaching and his intercourse with h
boys on to a new basis. It can, and should, colour all the subjects
his work in class. Of course he must be thoroughly competent pro
fessionally, but when that equipment is assured, it has seemed t
me that he goes on to a deeper and wider influence through the grac
of Holy Orders.

As a Headmaster I was glad to have the last appeal to a boy
conscience and character belonging to myself. A school chapla
can do very much, but he cannot be a substitute for the Head. View
differ on these points; no one can insist on his own opinion, nor h
he any right to tie the hands of governing bodies in their selection
a Headmaster. When I was a boy most Headmasters were ordaine
this is no longer the case. The number of laymen at the head of o
schools is far larger than the number of clergymen. I only mentio
my own predilections for what they are worth, and I believe that
far from the boys, if they think about it, feeling that a clerical Hea
is remote from common life, and has something artificial and form
about him, some of them have an instinct that they can look for a
claim the special help he has to offer.

When my ordination drew near, I stayed in the hospitable house
Canon Bernard at Salisbury, with its beautiful garden reaching dov
to the river. He had undertaken personally to examine me in all n
subjects, including Greek and Hebrew. The Bishop of Salisbury,
I have said, recognizing my special position and my engagements as
schoolmaster, was good enough to allow me to spend my summe
holidays in completing my studies at Auckland Castle with Bish
Westcott, and at the end I presented myself to Canon Bernard, waiti
to be ordained in the following Advent. A good many candidat
were ordained at the same time, but I do not remember the 'retre
as being very helpful; I had a considerable sense of nervousness a
hesitation, tension, diffidence, and unworthiness.

I myself discontinued at Norwich the practice of having lectu

EARLY YEARS OF BERTRAM POLLOCK

At the age of 3½.

At the age of 7.

BERTRAM POLLOCK WITH THE BISHOP OF DURHAM

elivered to the candidates on the day or two before their ordination.
here are not very many curacies in the diocese of Norwich in these
ays to which men can be ordained. One reason that has prevented
ie number being larger is that on the whole the clergy comprise
wer of the well-to-do men who in earlier years would have
rengthened the work and helped themselves in their later life by
iviting young men to join them in their parochial activities. Such
iracies might, in those days, be in the country. It is a mistake to
ippose that it is only in a town that a young man acquires useful
xperience. He finds life in the country more intimate; he knows the
omes, and families, and the children one by one. He learns to be
ery careful, for the people hang together; a sharp word alienates
ot only the one who hears it, but is repeated to others and discredits
im. A blend of town and country experience in early days enriches
man's career. Where curates have been required in the Norwich
iocese, it has often been necessary for the men to be already in Priests'
rders, because where there are in one benefice more churches than
ne man can serve, a deacon's help is inadequate as he cannot, of
ourse, administer Holy Communion.

I found at the beginning that the candidates for ordination who
ime forward did not reach a very high standard, but as the years
ent on they became better and better. It is for a bishop himself
decide whom he will ordain. But the subject of the qualifications
f candidates frequently comes up for reconsideration among the body
bishops, because it is desirable that there should be some uniformity
standard without tying a bishop's hands. (At the moment of writing,
is question is again before the bishops.)

The bishops many years ago recommended that every candidate
ould hold a University Degree; to which rule I adhered ever after-
ards. This did not mean that all the candidates went to Oxford or
ambridge: the younger universities had their share of them. Many
these candidates received financial assistance from the diocesan
inds and a careful committee used to consider the case of each
iplicant, his spiritual qualifications, his mental equipment, and his
iancial position. If the committee accepted a candidate he would
me to me for an interview to see whether I approved of him. On
aster Even every year I used to welcome the whole number of those
ho were in training, and they spent some of the morning and after-
oon in services in the chapel, when I would address them, and, after
e had lunched together, while I would, in the garden, be having a
tle conversation with each man, the others would be strolling about
little groups or talking to chaplains and others who had come to
with them.

B

When the time of the ordination came I saw, of course, ea[c]
candidate separately: I would say to him that I was at his servic[e]
that I did not intend to provide any set instructions, for I thought th[at]
his previous preparation for meeting his various examinations ha[d]
been sufficient and that my wish was that he, with a thankful hear[t]
should be conscious of the near presence of the Lord. I wanted th[e]
candidates to feel completely at home and happier and more at ea[se]
than I had been at Salisbury, though I had received much kindne[ss]
there.

My remembrances of my own ordination make me the more ful[l]
to enter into the mind of one man who, when we went into the Cathedr[al]
at Norwich for the service, could not be found. He flinched at th[e]
last moment. When I saw him afterwards I only recommended hi[m]
to get a good holiday and come up again next time. It was not [a]
moment for a rebuke, only for sympathy. He had been overwroug[ht]
by the stirring occasion.

I would motor the candidates about with me to any suitab[le]
engagement that I had planned beforehand and talk to each of the[m]
as we went along. In this my wife helped me, adding the touch [of]
personal welcome; for in October, 1928, the Archbishop of Wal[es]
married Joan Ryder and myself. She was the fourth daughter of th[e]
Rev. Algernon Dudley Ryder (a member of the Harrowby family); [a]
noble and beautiful example of Christian life and courtesy.

To fill any vacant time I would ask the 'ordinands' to read th[e]
notable sermon of Bishop Butler on 'The Ignorance of Man', and [a]
friend would often join us when we came to talk it over together. [I]
hope that all this made a happy and refreshing time for the candidat[es]
and led up to the ordination in a way that a series of lectures cou[ld]
scarcely have done. On the Saturday the candidates would mak[e]
the usual declaration:

*I assent to the Thirty-nine Articles of Religion, and to the Book [of]
Common Prayer, and to the Ordering of Bishops, Priests, and Deacon[s].
I believe the Doctrine of the Church of England, as therein set forth,
be agreeable to the Word of God: and in Public Prayer and Administrati[on]
of the Sacraments I will use the Form in the said book prescribed, an[d]
none other, except so far as shall be ordered by lawful authority.*

It is very important that whenever this declaration is mad[e]
whether before ordination or institution, it should not be regarded [as]
a legal formality, and that the man making it should make it with [a]
full sense of personal responsibility.

No man is bound to be ordained in the Church of England; b[ut] f he chooses to be ordained in it he must be ordained on the terms which the Church of England sets out. These he accepts, and it is or him to be loyal to his own declaration: he ought not to have a eeling that he has been, as it were, entrapped into using a mere form of words that does not really touch his head or his heart. There ought ather to be in his mind a sense of privilege in being accepted for Holy Orders or sent forward to a new post by the Church of England. There s no reason to suggest to a young man that later on he may change his mind. It should be his hope that as the years go by and his experience grows, and he reads more and more of the grand traditions and outlook of the Church of England, he will come to love it and its eaching and worship more sincerely and deeply as he understands hem better. If, later, doubts do occur in his mind he is wise for the ime being to keep them to himself, consulting those set over him who can help him. He would make a great mistake to preach about his misgivings to a general congregation.

The Church of England is generous and patient in its requirements and the actual wording of this declaration was modified eighty years go so as to give some latitude in the matter and to avoid a verbal igidity. If, in the end, on a broad common-sense view, it becomes lear to a man that he can only adhere to his promise by interpreting t in some artificial manner which would carry no conviction to anyone lse, it would appear to be at least difficult for him to exercise his office which was given to him on the clear and definite terms that he now ejects. He goes forth to his work as a pledged man, standing on firm round which the people can understand; they do not expect him to e a pioneer in ideas of his own, though, all the time, he can apply he old truths freshly to new situations. He is, in the words of the ld Latin, to teach *non nova sed nove* ('not fresh items, but in a fresh nanner').

I used to speak to the candidates along these lines, encouraging hem and congratulating them.

(I have appended at the end some words of mine to this effect ppearing in a book entitled *Holy Communion*, published by John lurray, 1917.)

I would sometimes use similar language to all this when I instituted clergyman in public to his new benefice, though then the main part f my address would relate to the co-operation of the clergyman and he people, and would remind them that here was no case of just a rofessional step in a man's career, but that the call had come from above.

I may say, in passing, that I generally instituted a man privately t the Palace, unless there was a particular reason for going to the church. It is often considered that the Bishop himself should be seen to send every man to his new work with his God-speed. In any case the Archdeacon inducts in the church, and if the Bishop is not there for the previous institution the Archdeacon can speak with good effect and, equally with the Bishop, he can point out the great care the Church of England tries to take to see that a good and sound man is appointed. It may seem unfortunate if the Archdeacon is silenced and if the whole diocesan weight is concentrated on the one first service in which the new incumbent appears. The Bishop can, on a subsequent date, go over and address the people when they know more of their new clergyman and he knows more of them.

When we returned after the ordination service to lunch, I always read the opening lines of Dr. Neale's translation of the beginning of the great poem of Bernard of Cluny (1145), *De contemptu mundi*, 'The world is very evil' (*Hora novissima, tempora pessima*). The Latin is a triumph of versification. The poem is easy to follow, for its thought is not progressive but eddies round and round the description of the celestial country. Those who heard it twice or oftener, fell under its spell. I did not ask any of the newly ordained to read, but read it all aloud myself.

I found at my own ordination at Salisbury that it was very embarrassing for a book to be passed round the table and read at meals: curiously few persons can read aloud in a room clearly and audibly. Some, no doubt, when their turn came to stand up and read felt nervous. I did not make a practice of reading aloud at the other meals during the retreat, but tried to guide the conversation into useful channels; I used to avoid having guests from outside. Once I remember, I felt rebuked. The third Lord Leicester, a great friend of mine, was in Norwich, and I invited him to lunch, with some fear that the conversation might become far away from the subject that was filling all our minds. It worked out very differently, and the young men received an indirect but eloquent sermon on practical considerateness. We were speaking of circulars from firms suggesting marvellous investments to their customers. Lord Leicester remarked that he tore them all up into little pieces before throwing them into the waste paper basket. "Why do you do that?" "Well, you know we have a great many housemaids at Holkham, and I am afraid that one of them might read the circular and be tempted to waste her wages in an investment of the kind."

CHAPTER VI

Edward VII

IN MY EARLY days at Wellington I reflected upon any special assets that the school possessed. The numbers had fallen and at the beginning of my time it did not really pay its way. We needed to attract more boys and to make the most of any advantages with which the school was endowed. It appeared to me that the school possessed quite an unique body of Governors.

The Prince Consort had taken the closest interest in the foundation of the school, and members of the Royal Family in the next generation had followed in his footsteps. It was wise to make the most of their connection with the school and I set myself to induce these important personages—with some of the other eminent Governors—to visit the school and personally to interest themselves in its welfare. I wanted them to feel that they were consulted and that their advice and sympathy were valued.

I ought to call attention to the manner in which the Governors are appointed. There are three or four *ex officio* Governors: all the others are co-opted, and then approved by the sovereign. They were men of distinction, and were not nominated to represent special interests. Each contributed his own experience, and they knew one another. The result was that they formed a brotherhood with no axes to grind individually, and could happily work together as a team simply set on promoting the good of the school. King Edward VII, then Prince of Wales, was the President of the Governors, and I remember that one day he said to me: "I think that you must find many things which require to be adjusted." He had visited the school on the Speech Day before I took over, and I was told that he had voted the visit with its time-table requiring an early start from London to be a bore. I felt that this would never do, and afterwards he paid many agreeable visits.

When King Edward was President of the Governors he had the welfare of the school at heart even in little things. I remember when he suggested a small change in the boys' dress he remarked to me: "Do not announce that the present practice has been abolished, say it is discontinued"—a little, but very wise, hint. He used to suggest to many of his friends to send their boys to Wellington. One could not fail to observe 'the good heart' he had, to quote the phrase of one of his family. I recall an occasion when the daughter of one of

his friends who had sent her boy to Wellington at his suggestion ha
caused much distress to her mother when she attended a drawing
room. Apparently she suffered from a kind of stage fright. Earl
next day, which was our Speech Day, I had heard from her mothe
asking me to suggest the name of a doctor to attend the poor gir
As soon as the Governors arrived they were full of the girl's behaviou
overnight and criticized it as a matter of general interest, for man
of them had been present. The King was the last to arrive and h
mentioned to me what had happened, saying that the girl had passe
in front of him and the Queen waving her arms like a windmill: the
he added: "Perhaps it was to steady her balance." It was, of course
a very far-fetched excuse, but I did not fail to notice that among th
many things that had been said about the incident his was the onl
remark that expressed any sympathy with the girl.

He would show his charming friendliness and again his goodnes
and kindness in setting those at ease who were presented to him. A
old colleague of mine whom I presented to His Majesty, not in a lon
row with a number of other people, but as he stood by himself where th
King was to pass, was obviously diffident. With his quick insight th
King saw that the only thing for my friend was to take his mind of
himself, so when I said: "May I present Mr. X, who has taught me al
I know about schoolmastering," he promptly said: "Then I congratulat
you, Mr. X, on having such an apt pupil." The awkwardness was gon
in a moment, for the minds of both of them were turned to me, and my
old colleague found quite at his ease.

One year, though the whole scheme had been carefully arrange
with his approval beforehand, I had carelessly omitted to put a pro
gramme of the proceedings in the place where the King was sitting
behind a table with the prizes upon it: two or three times he though
that it was the right moment for him to speak, and I had to whispe
to him that it had not yet come. It was planned that the head-boy
at the end of the prize-giving, should come forward and, turning hi
back on the prize table, should call: "Three cheers for His Majesty
the King, President of Wellington College." At the very momen
when it was impossible for me to signal to the boy, the King bega
to rise from his chair with these words: "And now I will speak." Thi
would have created a most unfortunate confusion. There was not a
second to stop the boy, and therefore, knowing that the King woul
understand, I ventured to restrain, with my elbow dug firmly into Hi
Majesty's ribs.

On one occasion he came to the dedication of a War Memorial o
the old Wellingtonians who had laid down their lives in South Africa
and he unveiled it. I explained to Sir Dighton Probyn that it woul

e impossible to have such a service without a short sermon. He
plied: "You can preach for five minutes, but no more." I did preach
r just less than three minutes. I cannot remember any sermon
hich gave me so much trouble, because it became necessary to speak
most entirely in monosyllables.

One time King Edward with Queen Alexandra lunched in a large
all with many distinguished guests. Again I was puzzled. With
reat trouble we had got the exact drink that he liked through the
eople at Windsor Castle, from which he drove over. By an accident
e upset the tall glass, spilling the whole contents on to the floor.
his figure had been more slight his legs would have been drenched,
ut most fortunately the plentiful contents of the tumbler poured
own between his legs without a drop splashing on to them. It did
ot seem that it would be polite to do nothing in an unpleasant situa-
on. With his usual good humour when I quickly knelt down with a
apkin as if to mop His Majesty's knees, he made everything easy
y saying: "Oh, that is nothing, thank you."

One day he created a diversion with his loud guttural voice. I
ad a garden party at my house and, calling to me, he said: "I do not
ke the caps the boys are wearing." (No one did.) I did not mention
at he had specially approved them some years before. "The boys
ould look better in wideawakes." The Duke of Connaught, seeing
look of surprise on my face, turned to his brother and said: "You
on't mean wideawakes, but bowlers." "Of course I was wrong,"
e Prince of Wales (as he then was) said, "I meant bowlers;" and
peated the word over and over again. It exactly suited his thick
oice, and the other Princes joined in. The Duke of Cambridge and
rince Christian were there—and they all roared with laughter and
outed the word. People at a little distance could not guess what
ould have come over the Royal group.

Prince Christian, by the way, once came over on a crowded day
r lunch. He slipped and fell down in the polished hall, when no
e at the moment was about. We ran and helped him up as he rubbed
is back. In the evening my housekeeper said to me: "I was upstairs
eping over the banisters and saw him fall down, and all I said to
yself was: 'Well, I wonder what you said when your eye was shot
ut?'" (The Prince, years before, had lost his eye in a shooting
ccident, and wore rather a fierce glass one.)

When King Edward paid such a visit to the College it was naturally
esirable to notice when he had had enough of the ceremonies, and
s soon as this was apparent, to make it easy for him to start home-
ards by simply ignoring the rest of any proposed programme. By
is goodness new pictures of himself and Queen Alexandra had just

been painted and they were on view in a little room near the grea
gateway from which he would leave. The pictures had been touche
up and slightly improved and adjusted by our excellent drawin
master who, I felt sure, would appreciate the honour of showing the
to the King. They did serve a useful purpose, for a large number
the members of the Royal Family had arrived before the King, wh
had come rather late. They had stepped, a little group at a time, int
the room where were the drawing master and the pictures, and th
had served to pass the time, especially as King George V (then Prin
of Wales), on hearing that the artist himself thought that they we
not well placed for exhibition, had made a humorous remark, sayin
that the artist was quite right, and that they would be better place
with their faces to the wall. This little jest was repeated to the othe
again and again and it was not taken amiss by anyone. The dreadf
thing was that when the King was to leave I forgot all about th
drawing master, who had the chagrin of watching from the window the
Majesties leaving without exchanging a word with him. I was s
penitent that the same night I wrote explaining what had happened an
asking that at some Speech Day in a later year, as soon as possible, th
King would again honour us with a visit. He came two years afte
wards, and I placed the drawing master in a small lobby through whic
the King would have to pass, and there full amends were made for m
carelessness. The King engaged in a friendly little chat with th
victim of my previous fault.

He was always very kind to me on these occasions. I remembe
once when he came to our Speech Day soon after he had won th
Derby (a very human interest which brought him near to the people
that he very graciously received my little allusion to it when I sai
that the King could not only present prizes but win and receive then
One time as we were walking across the Speech Hall he remarked t
me that the Prime Minister had been with him that morning and ha
recommended me for high ecclesiastical preferment. But I said t
him, "we cannot spare him"; though later on it was by King Edward'
direct interposition that I came to the See of Norwich, where I wa
better placed than in a distant northern Bishopric. When he ha
made the appointment I was told that he observed that if the Churc
of England were ever put into a position of serious difficulty I woul
come to the rescue. Here, for once, his insight was at fault, bu
his words revealed the kindness of his disposition, as did his previou
appointment of me as Chaplain in Ordinary, and the bestowal on m
of a C.V.O. when I was at Wellington.

(A few years later King George V graciously promoted me t
K.C.V.O.)

To his capacity for forming quick estimates of personalities was due some of King Edward's appeal in his private and public life. The spell which he cast over the French people was a case in point. At the beginning of his visit to Paris their welcome was reserved, but day by day his popularity grew, till at the end of his stay, in half earnest they declared, so the story goes, that if he had remained another week among them they would have made him King of France.

At home he was able, by his understanding, to bridge the gap between the old and the new nobility by welcoming the latter to his friendship. He was a great man, with a good heart, ready insight, and an unselfish sympathy.

CHAPTER VII

The Duke of Connaught

HE DUKE OF CONNAUGHT was removed during the course of the War. He was over ninety years of age when he died. He had many friends, for there was something very attractive in his disposition; but he belongs to the Victorian age and there are not very many people now living who were closely acquainted with him in public and private life.

It would be a mistake if those who belong to younger generations knew nothing about him, and it is right that those who knew him well should share their records, even if they have said or written something of the same kind before to those who are now looking forward to a new world which they will create, and who are naturally not given to mere retrospects of the past.

In men like the Duke we have certainly a heritage of which we may be proud, and it would be an impoverishment of our outlook upon the future if we disclaimed any connection with the great men of a bygone age.

It has not been easy in our English history to feel that we owe a great debt to the royal figures of the past; one has only to think of the unsatisfactory reputations of the uncles of Queen Victoria: but in the Duke of Connaught there was nothing to remind us of them, and I claim to put on record some of my own reminiscences with the intention of making the connection between the past and the

B*

future closer than it might be placed in the self-confidence of thos
who forget what they have owed to such men in the development o
English life.

There may have been some advantage in having at the head of th
Army one who, as a Royal Prince, was, so to speak, socially a bigge
man off duty when he had finished the day's work, and from whos
presence unauthorised persons could be excluded. But it wa
necessary to move with the times and not to concentrate so muc
power into the hands of one Commander-in-Chief, however dis
tinguished a soldier he might be.

Annually the Sovereign presents a gold medal to one of the boy
at Wellington College. With the presentation the terms of the awar
are read aloud: they inculcate "cheerful submission to superiors
good-fellowship with equals, independence and self-respect with th
strong, kindness, the protection of the weak, a readiness to forgiv
personal offences and to conciliate the differences of others, and
above all, fearless devotion to duty and unflinching cheerfulness.
It is added that "he who displays all or any of these qualities wi
have, so far, trod in the steps of the great Duke." There is reaso
to believe that these noble words were written by Lord Derby, th
Premier: the touch of the scholar is combined with the experience o
the man of affairs in this fine characterisation.

The Duke of Connaught, as a small boy, was with his mother o
a visit to the College. When he heard these words he exclaimed
"Where are his steps? I want to tread in them." Anyone who read
these words carefully, and sets by their side the character and th
achievements of the Duke of Connaught's full and protracted lif
will consider that the small child's ambition was richly fulfilled.

It was at Wellington that I first had the good fortune to meet th
Duke of Connaught. The Prince of Wales, later King Edward VII
was attending the annual Speech Day as President of the College
he regularly took the chair at the meetings of the Board of Governor
for his father, the Prince Consort, with Lord Derby, had first conceive
the founding of the school as an ever-*living* memorial to the Iro
Duke. The Duke of Connaught became the President of the Colleg
after his brother vacated the post on his accession to the throne.

Year by year the Duke never missed the opportunity of visitin
the College and addressing the boys; with all the long years of devote
public life and service his words carried all the authority of his ow
high ideals. His affability, his sense of the amusing side of thing
his cheery laugh, his delightful charm of manner won all hearts.

Little things are an indication of character. I remember on on
ceremonial occasion King Edward VII came over to Wellington wit

Queen Alexandra in the early days of motors, and arrived very dusty after the run. The Duke of Connaught had come before lunch and had washed his hands in my own room. King Edward remarked that he would like to have a wash to get rid of the dust. I was then a bachelor, and it was not possible for me to leave Queen Alexandra there and then. I was aware that the whole of my small staff (except a scullery maid) was on the lawn preparing for a garden party. In a moment the Duke turned to his elder brother and said: "Come along, I will show you the way. I know the Master's room." My horror was great on getting to my room—as soon as ever I could disengage myself from the gracious Queen—just in time to hear the Duke of Connaught saying to the scullery maid in a kind but firm voice: "And now you can go." I never knew, of course, what had taken place in the room where she stood, entirely unsupported, with the King and His Royal Highness. But the Duke, with his readiness to help me by relieving me of a puzzling position, must have entered into her feelings too, and like the true gentleman that he was, carried off the situation to the satisfaction of all persons concerned—even my own and the maid's.

As a speaker the Duke was simple and effective. But what a picture of selflessness and courtesy it was when, later in life, he came over to Wellington from Bagshot to the Speech Day: his infirmities made it impossible for him to stand while speaking and handing the books to the prize-winners. Most men who had been of smart and upright appearance in their active days would have shrunk from being seen in public at a disadvantage. Not he; his love for the school and his sense of duty towards it overcame any self-consciousness.

In later life he had come to fear that the old tradition of sacrifice and devotion to the country's good was fading in some directions. He felt it incumbent upon him quietly but effectively to keep bright by his words and influence the generous ideals to which he himself paid homage.

This desire to strengthen the principles of the rising generation led him one summer to accept many invitations to attend Speech Days at various schools in order to address the boys: it was just like him to feel that it was his special opportunity to help boys of the younger generation to appreciate the great heritage that had come down to them from the past and to do their part in carrying it forward to their successors.

CHAPTER VIII

Sidelights on Wellington College

ONE OF THE duties which the Governors of the College discharge i
to elect boys on to the Foundation. When the Duke of Wellingto
died it was decided that the money subscribed for a memorial to hir
should be spent on educating the orphan sons of officers. Some fou
hundred acres were bought and the College was built. It was a fin
idea that the great soldier at his death should be commemorated b
a college founded for the education of living boys to prepare them fc
manhood and service. The rules about the admission of Foundationer
have been modified from time to time. But in effect about a hundre
young boys, being the orphan sons of officers, are admitted t
Wellington College at largely reduced fees proportionate to the mean
of their widowed mothers. They can be accepted when they ar
quite little chaps of nine or ten years old. These are sent to variou
preparatory schools selected by the Headmaster and mothers ti
they are old enough to join the College. Some of these boys are chose
at an age when they can immediately enter the school. Man
preparatory schoolmasters valued this profitable connexion with th
College. One day the Master who helped me in this work receive
from the mother of a boy placed at one of these schools an effusiv
letter of gratitude thanking the Headmaster of it for all his goodnes
to her boy and saying regretfully that she was going to ask for hir
to be removed to a district that would better suit his health. Plainl
the letter reached us by mistake, posted in the wrong envelope
Next day the other letter was sent on to us by the Headmaster. I
it the mother implored me to change the school because she had foun
the Headmaster a most unsatisfactory man.

The boys on the Foundation mix freely with the other boys fror
all kinds of homes. No one draws any distinction between the tw
sets of pupils or knows them apart. It was one of my tasks to hel
in the examination of these very young boys. Sometimes m
dealings with them led to amusing or pathetic incidents. From ther
I learnt that the marriages of Henry VIII made a very strong appeal
if a little boy knew nothing about this king, who has been called "th
great widower", he would know no English History at all. One da
I had left behind me my easy reading book which I usually put befor
the candidates to read aloud. I was in the School Library and lookin
up I saw *The Life of Bishop Blomfield*. Opening the book I found

paragraph beginning with the words: "The good Bishop was loved by all who knew him." Little did I dream what was to follow. The passage went off into a description of the failures owing to drink which marked some few of the clergy of his day. I thought it would call attention to the passage if I interrupted, and I had no idea of the illustrations that were to follow! The little boy at the moment under examination read very well, and I thought it better to leave the matter alone, and that the mothers present would take anything that was being read as a matter of examinational routine. I hope I was right, though I was sorry to hear of a drunken clergyman carried away from the Bishop's table, and of another who at a funeral had fallen back into the grave that had been dug for the corpse. I chose the passage for the next boy with more care.

One day I was summoned from my class by hearing that a sobbing lady wished to see me. I quickly joined her. In her tears she told me that she was miserable because her boy was to be expelled from his preparatory school for stealing. I tried to console her and begged her to tell me the whole story. The boys of the school had been taken to an entertainment in a neighbouring hall. On their return, having missed their tea, each was provided with a bun and a glass of milk. The boy whose place at table was next to her small son was ill and absent, so he being hungry took the second bun with its glass of milk. She told me of the step she had already taken in asking a legal cousin to interview the Headmaster when "high words were spoken." I could not suppose that the schoolmaster would go through with his threat and it was far better that the thing should settle itself without my own interposition. He would have been sorry to lose my patronage of his school. She asked me what she was to do and I said "Nothing".

"Shall I bring my cousin to see him again?"

"Certainly not."

"Am I simply to wait and see?"

"Yes."

"May I write to you and tell you how the matter goes on?"

"By all means."

"Thursday is the day selected for his public expulsion."

For the next few days she wrote to me constantly and telegraphed, but all that she had to communicate was that nothing had yet happened. After a few more days I got a reassuring telegram: *Bun business blown over*.

It was a very sad occasion when it became necessary to remove from the school a boy who had stolen money. This is an offence for which boys have no forgiveness, however much I might have wished to give such an unfortunate boy another chance. This was a pitiful story, and unlike the usual case of a thief being a well-to-do boy who could easily have obtained money by writing home, this particular boy's mother was in very poor circumstances. I could not myself speak tenderly to her, for this would have been misunderstood by her and she would have supposed that I was vacillating and would yield to her entreaties. So I asked the tutor of the boy to write a gentle letter of sympathy over his own signature, that she might know that at any rate there was one among us who did feel for her distress. He did not quite take my meaning, and I said: "Would it save you trouble if I wrote a letter and you copied it out in your own handwriting?" He gladly assented and in a few days received this reply: "I can never thank you enough for your beautiful letter which went to my heart and has comforted me in all my misery. I do value your sympathy. As for the Master, he is a cruel man and I knew there was no hope of his showing the least mercy or consideration towards my poor boy and me."

At the end of every term it is usual for a written report on each boy to be forwarded home so that three times a year his position is reviewed. These three breaks caused by the holidays have the great advantage, to some extent supported by such reports, of giving a boy the chance of making a fresh start and of freeing himself from undesirable habits or friendships. (Many people would be the better for such opportunities in later life.)

Schools issue their reports in various styles: some Masters write a full letter to the father of the boy. More generally the report is formulated in a tabular form starting with the average age of the division in which the boy is placed. This is apt to be misleading, because one or two very old boys affect the average and make a boy seem to stand higher than in reality he does. Then will come a list of subjects, and the Master who instructs him in each of them writes his own comment, for many boys are taught each of his subjects by a different man. It is unfortunate that this plan, good in many ways, has displaced the form-master of earlier times who, teaching several subjects to the same boy, was better able to give a general review of his work. In all our educational plans there is the risk of regarding a boy or girl as a pupil in this or that subject and thus reducing the training of the whole personality. We are becoming the slaves of specialism, and are sacrificing individuality, if the boys are only thought of in their groups for instruction.

It was my business to read all these reports when completed, including the final remarks of the tutor or house-master responsible or watching the conduct of the boys in his 'house'. It was necessary to have someone to edit the completed record. There might be slips, and a Master would not always read what another had said in the line above his own. I recall the case of a boy who was the son of a Master. The report, intended to pay a compliment to a colleague, simply said "Like father like son": but the line above had stated "ignorant and futile". Again, I remember a tutor writing as an instructor saying: "Quite satisfactory with the exception noted below". In his report as tutor or housemaster he wrote below "ignorant and ill-behaved"— the exception appeared entirely to spoil the "Quite satisfactory" written above!

As I was doing this work my mind would sometimes go back to my own school days, and the thought of my father's attitude to the reports sent to him of my own performance would prevent me from exaggerating the importance of the long task I was doing. Perhaps he thought he knew me as well as my masters could and was satisfied. Perhaps his own experience of school life long ago came into his mind. The whole idea of school was different in those days. His mother died when he was six years old and he was sent off to school. When he was eight he turned to his father, a very busy man, and said he thought he ought to go to another school. My grandfather said he had better talk the matter over with his friends and others and choose a school. He did so and at the end of the term the account arrived. My grandfather looked at it and said: "So you have gone to the school of Dr. so-and-so." "Yes," replied my father; on which my grandfather said: "I wish I had understood that: I knew him years ago and I could have given you a letter of introduction to him." This is a wonderful tale when one thinks of all the care now spent in choosing the very right schools for boys and girls; but how well the boys, or many of them, in those days turned out. The spirit of independence and personal initiative was strong in the subsequent lives of the best of them.

CHAPTER IX

Archbishop Benson

ARCHBISHOP BENSON WILL always be a central figure in the story of Wellington College. To me, in my early years, he meant very much, and was a dominant influence in my life. It is with an affectionate gratitude that I draw a sketch of him as I knew him.

The Benson family has been prolific in its output of books. Arthur Benson wrote many volumes and there was a great sale for them in both England and America. There was a sweetness in his style and a fund of illustration, often humorous, that were very attractive. He wrote a long diary, of which the greater part is not to be published before fifty years have elapsed since his death. His brother Fred who for a short time was a pupil of my own, outlived Arthur by several years and went on writing to the end. He wrote novels and in his latter years produced some interesting work on the earlier Victorian era. One chief work of Arthur Benson was his *Life* of his father the Archbishop of Canterbury. It was long and elaborate and it gave a full account of his father's achievements and characteristics as he saw them. But I remember Bishop Stubbs of Oxford saying to me when he had read the book: "That was not the man I knew." Such a comment could be made concerning many biographies especially those that are as full of analysis as is this one.

I have read of a leading ecclesiastic speaking of Archbishop Benson as being aloof and a little-known figure of Victorian days, with whom few were intimate.

I may say that he has always occupied a vivid place in my own recollections. He was very kind to me as a young man and I often stayed with him. I can remember on a certain evening at Lambeth when I had arrived late and he came in later, his concern when he learnt that I had had a very meagre dinner before I reached the house: he left the room and shortly afterwards returned carrying a tray of refreshments for me with his own hand. Another time—in an influenza epidemic—in the early evening, he showed me a place in the famous chapel where I should be protected from all draughts during the service after dinner. There was something appealing in his considerateness, and there was an easy friendliness in his family circle. There was nothing pompous about him, and he would stay and talk when he ought to have been getting on with his letters. He was a man of great industry and took a very short night's rest. He would deliberately, five minutes before chapel-time, go to sleep for two minutes: like the Duke of Wellington, he must have been very tired to be able to do this. He would tell me about his early days at Wellington College, which, he said, were the happiest in his life. He would enter into the fun with his wife, who was an exceedingly clever and bright woman, when she put on his head a paper hat out of a cracker.

He much relied upon the guidance of one of his successors, Archbishop Davidson. They were men of a different stamp. Davidson was a man of immense experience. He had begun as chaplain to

rchbishop Tait, whose charming daughter he married. He was very
much interested in affairs and knew the ways of public life. Benson
once said of him that he enjoyed having his finger in every pie. Often,
t the end of his long life, after a debate in Convocation, Davidson
would, in his final words, take the matter back many years behind
he references of those who had been previously speaking. Davidson
knew exactly what to do in carrying out a course suggested by others,
but he had less aptitude for initiating a policy. He lacked indepen-
ence, and after opposing a resolution in the Church Assembly would
be ready, when it had been passed, to commend it to the House of
Lords. Being a devoted friend to the Archbishop he was most useful
in helping to guide and to give effect to the Archbishop's ideas.

Benson's mind was creative and it moved in the heavenly places.
here was a glow of poetry and scholarship in it. Yet he showed a
knowledge of the ways of men, as when he remarked that the best
method of forming public opinion was through private conversation.
Benson's knowledge of the Greek Testament, whose phrases he con-
tantly applied to questions of the day, was large and ready. Some
eople thought that when he came into London life there was some-
hing provincial in his outlook. Unlike Davidson, he never was quite
t home in speaking in the House of Lords.

Benson had a singular dignity of appearance, and his countenance
rew in beauty as the years went by. If he had been taller he would
ave had an even more impressive presence, and through all his life
e was a fine actor of noble parts. This was not a matter of pose or
elf-consciousness, for he was at his ease and not one of those who,
ot being sure of themselves, seem to take refuge behind a mask. He
would take the lead when it was right for him to do so, and no one could
e disappointed with his bearing. It is said that at a time when the
hurch of England was being exposed to severe criticism in a great
ity and the Archbishop was visiting that place in order to take part
n some conference, people were rather nervous about the reception
e might receive. The Lord Mayor received him at the station, and
s they drove through the street the Archbishop's demeanour was so
ull of grace and dignity, of courtesy and benevolence, that before he
eached the Congress Hall his charm had won the day.

He was not an effective writer. Prince Lee, afterwards the first
Bishop of Manchester, had among his pupils, when he was head-
master of the Birmingham school, both the Archbishop and Bishop
Westcott of Durham. He taught them both to eliminate every possible
word, with the result that their writings became obscure. In speech
Bishop Westcott corrected this fault by a glowing emphasis; the
Archbishop by the gesticulations he freely used. They were great

friends and, just as the Archbishop turned to Davidson for guidance in method, he turned to Westcott for guidance in thought.

Benson's weakness lay in his temper, when a heavy cloud would descend upon him and his face would fall. Much is said about this in his brother Arthur's biography. He probably felt it keenly; once writing to his wife that gentleness was the greatest power in the world. Probably this drawback was seen at its worst in his schoolmastering days. But against this must be set the fact that in some fifteen years by his creative genius he had transmuted an institution (which, as first planned by the Prince Consort along rather German lines, might have been just an orphanage for the sons of officers) into a great public school.

Queen Victoria was attached to him, for the school was the joint achievement of the Prince Consort and the Archbishop, who was appointed to be headmaster before the school was ready to be opened. The Prince had a high opinion of him and gave much attention to the working out of the life of the school.

The Archbishop inspired a devoted staff with his own enthusiasm. He held that the first duty of a headmaster was to teach and not to become only an organizer. He provided a hymn book for use in the chapel containing many hymns that he had himself composed as he walked in the woods, including the magnificent: 'O throned, O crowned with all renown.' He firmly believed in having a bookseller's shop attached to the school, instead of employing a clerk to take down orders for books. In the shop, boys could have good books before their eyes and learn something from the titles of new publications. He set a stamp upon the school which it has never lost. His readiness to apply the words of Scripture was illustrated in those days, when a new church was being built between Wokingham and Wellington College among the fir trees which have always been an adornment to the district. He took as his text the psalmist's words: "Lo, we heard of the same at Ephrata: and found it in the wood." Or on another occasion, when a National Day of Prayer was being proposed, he said, "We must be sure we do not fall into the error of praying to be seen of men."

A notable event of his episcopate was the judgment which he pronounced on the case brought against the Bishop of Lincoln concerning ritualistic practices. His knowledge of the points at issue and his elucidation of them won praise on all sides, and the Privy Council accepted his interpretation of the law. It is strange that so fine and careful a piece of work should be now ignored. The hearing of the case began in the afternoon, but no one could find the Archbishop during the morning. (It was characteristic of him to relax in small

ys if he needed a little rest from his incessant work, though when he
is on holiday he made a business of it all.) On this morning he was
scovered hanging pictures in a remote bedroom at Lambeth. I
en thought—during the debates on the revision of the Prayer
ook—what a misfortune it was that he was not there to guide the
shops: for he had the whole thing at his fingers' ends—to him, for
ample, the only Holy Gospel was the Gospel for the day. Yet
en some discussion on the forms of worship had been taking place
which he had shown his full and accurate knowledge, he would
ughingly say at the end: "But these are not the things of primary
portance." The appeal which the ancient Church of the Assyrians
ade to him for his support stirred his sympathy, with all his knowledge
early Church history.

He delighted in the class for prominent ladies which at certain
nes he used to hold week by week. It was as congenial to him as
he were instructing his Sixth Form. His boys sometimes exclaimed
at he would continue his enthusiastic lessons so long that he left
em only seven minutes for their breakfast, and he gave as his reply:
t is wonderful how much breakfast you can eat in seven minutes
you give your mind to it."

He designed a charming house at Wellington for the Master's
sidence, giving the boys an easy access to his study: the nursery
as a very attractive room. Once, when his son Fred came to see me
ere, he was surprised that he could recognize none of the pictures
om the *Illustrated London News* which his father had pasted on to
e wall, until his eyes dropped on to the lowest pictures just above
e wainscot, and there he recognized them all, because they corre-
onded to his stature when he was a child. Another very welcome
sit at Wellington was from the old nurse of the family who had
en with Mrs. Benson at Wellington, at Lincoln, at Truro, and at
ambeth. She was a very fine old lady and, I believe, in all his
vancements she steadily called him 'Sir'.

The first visit I paid to him was to Addington, where he took a
eat interest in the estate and the management of it (in the days of
s successor it ceased to be a country home for the Archbishops of
anterbury). A year or two later there was rather a serious matter
school management and discipline that I wanted to talk over
ith him. I explained the whole situation, and the rather bold and
nusual way in which I thought of handling it. Next morning he
ave me his views, but I have always respected the way in which,
ough he made no secret of the fact that he would have acted differ-
ntly from me, he made the fine remark: "The man who sees a course
f action is the man who can carry it through." He neither hampered

me nor hindered me, and I came away filled with gratitude and new strength.

He wrote a monumental life of Cyprian, and humorously he use to speak of it as his real occupation. It was a joy to him to be able do one piece of work in a thorough and scholarly style; so many his incessant labours had to be carried through without adequa opportunities for full and careful discussion and consideration. I kept a special Cyprian table, and when he had, or thought he had, little time to spare, he would do a little work on it. He began t Life when he was at Wellington, and continued it in all the yea that followed. His style does not make it very attractive readin but it was a wonderful contribution from an overworked Archbish to the History of the Church; and there are pregnant comments it on, for instance, the importance of consulting the laity on the mann in which desuetude can correct faulty decisions. The volume was ju finished in time to be published immediately after his death, whi occurred when he was the guest of Mr. Gladstone, journeying hom wards from his visit to Ireland, where he had won all hearts. On h way to Hawarden he attended the evening service in Carlisle Cathedra where he heard for his last anthem: 'Oh send out Thy Light and Th Truth, that they may lead me and bring me unto Thy Holy Hill an to Thy Dwelling.' What a beautiful translation for a beautiful lif

It had meant very much to me in my earlier years at Wellingto to know that he was behind me, and I was proud to be one of the pa bearers at his funeral in Canterbury Cathedral as the processio went up the nave thronged with mourners whose grief and affectio could be read upon their countenances.

CHAPTER X

School Discipline

WHEN I WAS appointed to the Mastership of Wellington College was one of the youngest members of the staff. The school had onl recently returned from Malvern, to which place it had gone int exile while the whole drainage system was being reorganized. Naturall at Malvern it had not been possible to maintain a full precision discipline, on which it is necessary to write a few preliminary word

I always found it impossible to predict, when I was engaging a assistant master, whether he would be able to keep order. Some en who seemed from their appearance, their record of sportsmanship d other things, certain to be successful, proved failures. Only ce did I feel quite sure: a poor, weakly-looking applicant came to e me. I was convinced that he would not do. A little later I had telegraph to a scholastic agency asking for a breakdown man to sent at once. To my dismay this particular man arrived. Before had been with us a week it was plain that he was a real disciplinarian d a good teacher. My one prophecy had miscarried! I have heard the same kind of thing in a village school in which the regular istress could not keep order satisfactorily. She had leave of absence r some reason, and a substitute mistress who replaced her reformed e school in two weeks.

No one will succeed who is not himself at ease in the presence of e boys he is to control, and no severity of punishment will cure sorder.

We had one most excellent drawing master, capable and kind-arted, but boys are quick to see a weak spot and to exploit it. He d the mistaken idea that punishment was the right weapon with hich to maintain discipline. When he was teaching drawing one y he had in the room with him a boy from a humble home in the ighbourhood who helped him to arrange his papers and so on. ne of the boys saw his chance and said: "May I ask your son, sir, hand me some paper?" Another day he was complaining to me the behaviour of boys who were throwing india-rubber about the om. I told him how dreadfully shocked I was to hear this, and he ade the naïve rejoinder: "Oh, but they were very little pieces."

Personality, not punishment, must confront boys, and they must arn that they are the losers in such a game. Unfortunately, per-nality cannot be acquired. Often a situation can be met by a nse of humour and by raising a laugh against a delinquent among s fellows. The same kind of thing can be used in handling a crowd.

One of my colleagues was fond of travelling in Greece, and he would ve so much to tell of his adventures that he would bore the boys ho came to his room. He offered to give a lecture on Greece to a hool society before which papers were read. The members of it were w, and each paid one shilling to join. When it became known that r. B. was going to speak one evening, the boys paid their shilling trance fee and joined by the hundred earlier in the day. Their ly idea was to 'rag' the man, to use their own phrase. I heard of e plan and attended myself. There was, of course, perfect order roughout. At the end I thanked the lecturer and mentioned that

the popularity of the speaker and his subject could perhaps be measure
by the fact that this very large number had joined the society o
purpose to attend: I said no word of censure, and the boys were goo
humouredly and delightfully annoyed with themselves and me.

There was a boy not well fitted for school life, but an engagi
little fellow, who one day appeared in my study saying his companio
had told him I wished to see him. I recognized the plot against hi
and said: "So I do; come and have some tea." Several people we
staying in my house, who quickly recognized that I wanted to mal
much of the boy. We fed him royally on birthday cake, and he soc
became quite at home and asked our help in suggesting a Christm
present for his father. Then I sent him off and told him to be su
and thank the others for sending him along. We became fast frienc

I wished to lead a liar to speak the truth and own up to son
fault. I was always eager not to punish a culprit before he had himse
acknowledged his fault. This was also a help if any question aro
later. It seemed better not to argue further with this boy and
said he was to wait in my garden while I was writing, and to come
every half-hour when the clock struck and repeat his denial of what
knew he had done: other boys were playing cricket. This he did a
the afternoon. At each appearance of his I made no remark. B
after this had gone on for four hours the boredom and the absurdi
of the situation wore him down and at last he confessed.

On another occasion the humour was quite unintentional. I ha
a delinquent before me, a charming boy who later became a very re
friend. I was sitting on a club fender in my study and sayir
unpleasant truths to him as they came into my head. A little fi
was burning, and a small upright screen stood in front of it. A c
was asleep at my feet. I leant back too far and suddenly the clu
fender, not being fixed, fell forward and just missed the cat, wl
gave a vertical spring into the air. I fell backwards and the scree
saved me from sitting in the fire. I broke the poker as I went b
But I soon recovered myself and throughout the incident I did n
pause a moment in my discourse. I can now see the look of bewilde
ment on the boy's face. All was as it was a minute before, but ther
was the agitation of the cat, and the broken poker! What a story l
had to tell when he rejoined his friends!

There were one or two whole holidays in the year, and immediatel
after morning chapel the boys went off to the station to catch the
train. All had to pass my seat as they went by. Some of them woul
put on bits of holiday dress, which was irregular in the chapel.
would say to these: "Wait a minute for me outside." When I di
come out, knowing exactly how long it would take a boy to come bac

me wearing the right tie and then run off and change it again into
the holiday tie, and finally run to the station, I would keep him waiting
while I spoke to a colleague. The boys who did this caught the train,
but it was a useful reminder of rules. Any graver misconduct was
often dealt with in a similar way at the end of term. A boy would
be sent for to see me after breakfast and I would then tell him I was
busy for the morning and he could come back before lunch. The
other boys had left at 7 a.m., and he had a very dull and desolate
morning. At the end of it, the incident closed with a good-humoured
word or two from me.

Occasionally time was saved and a boy's sense of humour touched,
, when he was referred to me for bullying, I took the words out of his
mouth and said before asking any question: "Let us be agreed on
this, that whatever you have done, it was nothing like what was done
to you when you first came here; and also you did not know that he
minded it." If a boy ran away from school I usually made it a condition that, if he returned, the responsibility for the future should rest
with his father, and that he should bring back a doctor's certificate
saying it was safe for him to come back. I was puzzled once when the
doctor reported that a certain boy ought to be 'punished impressively
but not severely'. I sent for him and in the presence of a number of
school prefects I gave him a long address and some very paltry
punishment.

I must conclude these disjointed remarks with a comic but pathetic
story: In my early days I found a tendency to disorderliness, and one
day live matches were thrown on to the floor of the chapel, and a
master going out let them off as he stepped on them. Quite a fusillade!
The culprits did not give themselves up, and, knowing that if a wholesome and general public opinion had condemned the thing as silly,
it would not have been done, I inflicted some general punishment. A
boy came to see me and begged me to punish him severely in the matter.
"It is you, then, who did this?" I asked. "No," he said; "but the
others think I did, and I would sooner be punished by you than
rough-handled by them." I declined. (Strangely enough, this boy
was the son of the artist who had painted a well-known and pathetic
picture of the *Scapegoat in the Wilderness*.)

It is, I think, a mistake to try and cow boys with a distant severity.
Meet them on their own ground; let them see that you understand
what is in their mind, and that you know they understand what is
in yours. Such mutual understanding, flavoured with a little humour,
will all make for a good-tempered response.

Silence I found a most useful instrument for discipline. Until I
had mentioned what his punishment was to be, a boy who had gone

wrong, conjured up in his mind every kind of far-fetched possibili
and pictured something much worse than was my actual decisio
given after a long delay. His own imagination provided a mo
painful scourge than I possessed. This is in human nature and h
its counterpart in many ways in the larger world.

CHAPTER XI

Punishment

DISCIPLINE AND PUNISHMENT are, in the minds of many peopl
closely, perhaps too closely, associated, and if as a schoolmaster
had some ideas on the subject of discipline, I have long reflecte
carefully upon the difficult issues involved in the question of punis
ment in its wider aspects, as it touches the life of a larger or small
community.

Before the war an important Bill was coming before Parliamer
with reference to changes in the Criminal Law. At the time the ve
important subject of the reformation of the accused person was beir
widely discussed. But there is a good deal more in punishment to k
considered than that one aspect of it.

Some years ago Lord Haldane, then Lord Chancellor, was speakir
to a gathering of magistrates assembled in Norwich; such an addre
from a Lord Chancellor was not unusual in those days. After th
meeting he came back to my house, and before his train there was tin
for some conversation and it turned to the subject of punishmen
This led on to some little correspondence between us on the matte
in which it was agreed that there were many aspects of the questio
to be weighed up.

To begin with it is generally accepted that one who does wror
must suffer for it. Is it too philosophical to speak of the majesty
Right and of the Law which upholds it? We often have this them
presented to us in the great Greek tragedies. Of course, when we spea
of law upholding right we must not do so in a pedantic way. Man
will remember the earnest letter which Miss Helen Waddell wrote t
The Times protesting against six young men being executed in Norther
Ireland for one offence of murder. Her plea prevailed. She wrot
as one who felt that, in his great play of Antigone, Sophocles had mad

clear that there is something above and beyond human enactments
which men must respect as superior to them.

We have to see that punishment is so enforced as to protect society.
This is rather more than saying that punishment must act as a deterrent
to others who may be led to pause before committing a crime, by having
before them the example of the punishment of some other person.
To this end the example and parallel must be perfect, exhibiting the
punishment of the self-same act. In the exchange of views that took
place when the new Bill was being considered, the Judges laid more
emphasis on this side of punishment than did those who could only
think of reformation. In regard to juvenile offenders, however, the
Lord Chief Justice has remarked that the idea that society had to be
protected against such persons should be renounced once and for all;
for they were often more the victims of what society had done, or
failed to do, than offenders against society.

There must be nothing vindictive in punishment. While we have
no desire to make things too easy for the guilty person, yet the punishment must not be excessive in proportion to the offence committed.
It may be that a revolt against the excessive punishments of old
days has carried public opinion too far in the opposite direction. We
are now shocked to think of a man being hanged for theft. It would
be very desirable if a punishment could be made to match the offence,
though undesirable if a man guilty of brutality were punished
brutally. There is a dignity in human personality and this must
not be forgotten even in the case of one who has degraded himself
to a low level of coarseness and cruelty in his actions towards others.

Where it is possible punishment should involve some restitution;
and there are cases in which one who has wronged another can give
back, if only partially, something of which he has deprived his victim.

When we think of the reformation of one who has done wrong,
we reach a most weighty point in the whole question, but we will
bear in mind that suffering itself may be an element in reforming
him. The Greeks wrote παθή ματα μαθή ματα (we learn from our
sufferings), and they were quite right; especially have we to be on
our guard against a perverted sentiment which makes a hero of some
disgraceful scoundrel, and forgets all about those against whom his
offence has been committed.

In dealing out punishment it is proper that we should act in such
a way that the offender understands what is being done. That is
the defence of a punitive expedition against a savage tribe. They
cannot be lectured and the only thing to bring them to their senses
is some retaliation of which they can apprehend the meaning. It is
difficult to determine at what stage a civilized community has fallen

so low that it can only be reached and improved by the same ki
of punishment that befits the savage and uncivilized. Again, th
justification which is found for a general punishment in which a who
society suffers with no distinction drawn between the apparent
innocent and the unspecified, or undetected guilty, lies, as I hav
suggested, in the fact that it would be in the power of 'the innocen
to check the offence or crime, by raising public opinion against anythir
of the kind, which would act as a deterrent. For it is in the acts
individuals that the outlook of the whole number is revealed.

In the infliction of punishment there must be a very defini
sense of responsibility felt towards all the parties and interests co
cerned in the matter. We cannot extend forgiveness to an offende
as if we had a right to let him go unpunished, in the way that we ca
forgive a personal injury. Such wisdom and commonsense as w
possess must be used in our judgments or we may find ourselves le
astray into theories about wrong-doing which will vitiate our practic
We shall, for example, make mistakes if we find ourselves arguin
that wrong actions are the result of some inherent force that make
a man *not* responsible for what he does. We have to recognize tha
we all possess free will and are not automata, which can exercise n
choice and responsibility against the pressure of Fate, or whateve
else we call it. The law has clear and well defined rules with referenc
to insanity and the border-land between sanity and insanity, and
Judge in summing up always makes them plain to the jury.

We may, no doubt, as our knowledge increases, one day form ne
views upon culpability and the punishment of it, but we have now t
handle the matter with such knowledge as at present we possess.

CHAPTER XII

Navy Examination

IT MADE A pleasant change from my routine work at Wellington whe
I was invited to be a member of one of the interviewing Boards wh
sorted out the small boys coming forward as applicants for the Navy
I was rather sceptical about the scheme when it was started, but afte
watching it at close quarters I entirely changed my mind. It ha

med to me that it would be impossible to obtain a real knowledge
the capacity of a boy if he was alarmed by meeting and speaking
th a number of men whom he must regard as very old and terrifying.
practice this was not the case. It was far easier than I had thought
allow for the shyness of a diffident boy, and it may be that a boy
twelve or thirteen was less self-conscious than one two years older.
yhow, on this occasion the system seemed to work. The whole
ing did not depend upon the interview, but the boys waiting to
me before us were given a short essay to write, and if they success-
ly got through the interview they had to pass a qualifying
amination. It was remarkable that the five of us who constituted
e Board always agreed in our estimate of a candidate. The matter
mere shyness was overcome by the geniality and sympathy of the
dmiral of the Fleet, Sir Arthur Fanshawe, our chairman, who would
ring up and shake hands with each boy as he entered the room and
ake him feel that he was among friends.

The system of admission has, I believe, been once or twice altered
ice then, but the system that I saw seemed to me to be fully satis-
ctory. Each of the examiners would take his turn in being the
st to question a little boy when he came in. It was a help that
turally the examiners came to know one another and the questions
) that each would put many times over again. We could guess
e impression that was being formed in the mind of each examiner
his questioning proceeded.

Before a boy came in there was read aloud to us the estimate of
m formed by his preparatory schoolmaster. These were perhaps
s helpful than they might have been, because they were apt to be
) long and effusive. It was amusing to see the way in which the
ath of the Admiral would again and again be stirred by the report
a schoolmaster who would write: "We all like him and he is popular
th his schoolfellows. He plays games well, but I am afraid that his
ain is not his strongest point and he is backward for his age, but he
a good sportsman, a thorough little gentleman, and just the boy
the Navy." The Admiral would exclaim: "Ours is the most
ientific profession, and we certainly don't want brainless boys
cause they have good manners." I represented nothing particular
the Board and often asked questions on common knowledge such
, "What is the price of such and such an article?" or I would ask
boy to read a little bit of French, or to recite some short bit of
etry that he had learnt. King Edward VIII was one of the
ndidates and with our usual unanimity we formed our estimate of
m, and I remember that we placed him second of the whole number.
me little fault in his Essay told against him for first place. I asked

him to recite a piece of poetry of his own choice, for I remembe
his grandfather telling me that on his birthday his grandsons k
recited to him in, I think, three languages. The little boy asl
whether it should be short or long and I chose the offer of a sh
piece. Immediately, without any awkwardness or hesitation,
recited Tennyson's *Crossing the Bar* with remarkable taste. It
probable that the whole examination was of a kind to suit him f
young as he was, he had mixed in the company of many differe
people and was easily at home with the members of such a board

In those days public criticism of written examinational tests v
rarer than it is to-day, and it may be that the efforts of these lit
boards that were constantly being set up by the Admiralty told
favour of the interview system now coming more prominently in
vogue. But human nature being infinitely varied does not le
itself to any one hard and fast plan, and we have only to think of c
able administrators and soldiers and empire builders, when the orc
of the day left the choice of them to private initiative. But t
examination system has cast the net wider and brings in so
candidates of whom personal patronage would never have hea
We have become more democratic. The Norwood Report, howev
deprecates the value at present laid upon external examination a
believes that the internal observation of pupils and aptitudes
preferable; teachers can themselves provide intelligence tests, t
judgments of teachers being of chief account. But as the n
Education Bill shows, we shall have to proceed with caution if '
try to offer a welcome into our Public Schools to boys who at prese
do not find their way there. There will be some selection and sorti
out to be accomplished and many points to be considered if we a
not to lose in this extension some of the very things which we ha
most prized in these schools, and in the contribution they have ma
to the Nation and Empire. I remember a school authority, fro
Norway, I think, paying a visit to Wellington in order to learn son
thing about our Public School system, but the imponderable thin
which make these schools what they are did not much interest tl
attractive guest of mine. The incidental training in leadership a
in the spirit of give and take; the rearing of future citizens; the gam
in which a boy finds his level; the gradations in that common life
which big and small are equally proud—these things meant little
one who chiefly regarded the boys as pupils for formal instructio

Another educational interlude came every year. I was an exami
ing chaplain to the Bishop of Lichfield and I paid a visit to the Pala
in the summer to interview and test the candidates for ordinatic
One day, I remember, there was an amusing occurrence: the Bishe

s away for the night and Mrs. Legge would not be returning from
engagement till very late. I was leaving early next morning and
vent to dine with friends in the Close. When I came in, I found
: butler, who was rather a character, in some anxiety concerning
young woman who had just arrived. He told me this story which
vould not have recounted here if I had not known from a mutual
:nd that the heroine of it had mentioned the incident. The young
ly in question had appeared at the Palace asking to see Mrs. Legge
i wishing to be taken in for the night. There had been some
sunderstanding on the part of herself or of her maid, and finally
: had been carried on in the train without the maid, and found
self at Stafford: I forget which was the station at which she ought
have got out. She had no friends at Stafford, but remembered
it Mrs. Legge had been at school with her mother. On the strength
this she came to Lichfield. The butler's suspicions were aroused
d he asked me whether he should keep her for the night. Was she
enuine lady? I replied that first of all she ought to have something
eat. This was brought up to her in the drawing-room, and I sat
d talked to her while she took it. It so happened that her refresh-
nt consisted of a poached egg and cherry tart—neither of them
y easy things to eat elegantly. But she was so successful that
ssured the butler that he need have no fears. A few days later I
ard from the Bishop that the story, however improbable, was true,
i that I had quite correctly estimated this unexpected visitor.

CHAPTER XIII

July

WILL OFTEN be found that the month of July is a trying month.
some senses it marks the end of the year in Church life and School
:. It is the month before the main holiday begins and, while
:ryone is looking forward to beginning again in October for the
tumn campaign, they find themselves tired out and lacking in
tiative in July, when the hot weather makes even the phlegmatic
patient and irritable.

At school I found it a difficult time. The elder boys who were
ving at the end of the term were beginning to be critical of their
sters, who had been their heroes in the earlier years. They were

looking forward to the freedom of the holidays, when they would
treated as young men, freed from the necessary small restrictions a
punctualities of school life. It has always seemed to me import
and yet unusual that a schoolmaster should treat even his youn
pupils with some of the respect that would be due to him a few ye
later; *"Maxima debetur puero reverentia,"* as the Latin phrases
But this particular mistake is not made by schoolmasters alone.

It is sad to observe the way in which Fathers and Mothers in
classes lose the confidence and affection of their boys and girls
treating them as still children when already they are making frie
and becoming important outside the home. Parents do well to k
up with the development of their children, remembering how ra
it is, and to welcome the new friends whom they have made.

I remember the opposite mistake being made by a small boy,
present Lord Carnock (son of Sir Arthur Nicolson as he then was,
famous ambassador). The boy was very seriously ill and his fat
and mother used to stay in my house to be near the sanatorium
visit him. One day Sir Arthur suggested a date to come, and I s
he would be very welcome, only *that* evening I would have with
our school XI, and the XI of another school who had come fo
two days' match. Good humouredly he said he would enjoy
Next morning, visiting his son, he almost caused a relapse when
mentioned that at supper he had sat between the head of one sch
and the captain of the other team.

Masters, too, had by July become tired of one another and tl
complaints concerning things in general were frequent and vocifero
I sometimes found that it was a good plan to listen to such co
plaints sympathetically, and then suggest that they should come b
about it in the autumn. The probability was that the subject wo
never be alluded to again.

At one time we had a German steward, and the day came when
had some quarrel with the chef and came to complain to me on
subject. I pointed out to him that though I was responsible for
whole management, it would be better if any serious complai
reached me through the Bursar. Mr. C. was the chief accountant
the Bursar's office, and the steward immediately replied to me: "I
no good saying anything to the Bursar, he is led by Mr. C.'s nos

This steward was a clever fellow, however: there was a wh
holiday one summer given on the occasion of some public functi
most of the boys had gone away to London and I arranged to ta
some fifty or so of them for a river excursion. The steward sa
"If I take a change of clothes with me may I raise the cry of 'M
overboard' after tea, when on these excursions people have rea

ıd enough of it and want a new excitement to keep them going?"
ne day I was shocked at the amount of brandy that was being used
. the kitchen and began to look into the matter myself, when I was
ıld by the steward that a long time previously one of the kitchen
ɔys had fainted and the school doctor had pronounced that there
as nothing like immediate brandy for such a case, and ever after-
ards a bottle of fresh brandy was always at hand.   This was like
ıe story of Queen Victoria who, it is said, was driving out in Windsor
ark when some careless and unsober driver met her and an uncom-
ʳtable accident was in prospect.   The Queen, not understanding
ıat the man had already had too much of such treatment, urged that
ɂ should be given some brandy.   There was none available, so Her
ajesty, it is said, gave the order that whenever she drove out in the
ternoon, a bottle of brandy should be taken in the carriage.

I remember another such excursion that I had to plan.   This
so was in the summer at the time of our annual Speech Day which
ing Edward was attending.   We had had a severe epidemic of
easles.   One did not ever dare to remit cautions against measles
hich in those years had taken on a severer type, but the very success
these precautions made the disease spread vigorously when once
got a hold and dangerous consequences would follow.   It would
ɪve been a terrible thing if the King had, through his visit to us,
ɂntracted the illness which, by that time, was past its peak; so I
ɔllected the boys who were still 'possibilities' and sent them on an
ɂcursion to the sea.   Three boys in this group actually developed
on the return journey.   This was probably a wise step to take, for
ɪe King's mother and his nurse were both dead and it was impossible
ɂ discover whether he had been a victim of measles in his childhood.
ıch epidemics are one of the trials of a schoolmaster's life.   Our
hool doctor was very good in dealing with them.   He used to come
ıd see me *every* morning.   I made this plan in order that his arrival
my house should not arouse suspicions or rumours.   Unfortunately,
he *was* anxious he would whistle as he went along.   My secretary,
ɪnouncing that he had come, would, if it was the case, add "And
ɂ is whistling".

I remember in the depths of winter, not in July, hearing that one
ʳ two cases of smallpox had occurred in the village on the edge of our
ɔllege estate, and for this pervasive illness it was necessary to make
ɔme severe restrictions.   We put a pensioner as sentinel at each of
ɪe many gates to the College grounds.   Providing each of these men
ıth materials with which to build himself a comfortable nest, I gave a
ıall prize to the one who did this best.   They allowed no one to enter
to the premises.   At one end of the grounds I secured a cottage in

case one of our boys fell ill. It appeared to be impossible and unsa
for smallpox to be nursed in any part of the large school sanatoriu
The matter was urgent and I went to see the occupant of this ve
delightful cottage and said to the owner: "If I give you such-and-su
a sum will you entirely clear out of the place and the house by mid-d
to-morrow?" She had no children, only a husband. She accept
the offer, and when I inquired whether it would be all right with h
husband she said: "He will be all right." Next day I returned an
finding the place ready and beautifully clean, I just asked what t
husband had said when he came home from his work on the previo
evening; and she pleasantly replied: "Oh, he was surprised." /
went well and the smallpox did not spread to the School.

No doubt things are planned better now, but in the hot summ
weather the boys used to go into School after their midday dinn
with the idea that they would play their games in the cooler evenin
but of course the afternoon lessons were very sleepy and I used oft
to carry off the class which I was teaching into my own garden. T
boys were very good about it and kept their eyes on their bool
relying on my promise that I would call their attention to anythi
exciting that might take place, such as a boxing match which son
prize cats of mine used to hold, sometimes staged on the lawn, to t
huge delight of the boys. Sometimes I would open the lesson in t
class-room by telling the boys to get it over and to sleep for ten minut
promising to call them when the time allotted to slumber was u

(If ever I myself fell asleep in class I was careful to rememb
my grandfather's habit if he slept on the Bench: when he woke
would keep his eyes closed for a while and then refer to somethi
said a few minutes before he opened them. The court might thi
he had heard everything, keeping his eyes shut for closer attentio

The difficulty of arranging summer hours is not confined to school
since the days of Mr. Willet it has been with us in town and countr
This summer time is generally applauded, but it has its difficultie
and now especially the double summer time in July. Some yea
ago a farmer wished to attend Morning Prayer at 11 a.m. His fami
comprised four persons: each of them had moved the clock by o
hour, with the result that he reached church at 3 p.m. when afternoo
service was about to begin, and he did not for some time discov
the mistake.

Edward R & I.

EDWARD VII AT BALMORAL

BERTRAM POLLOCK'S CONSECRATION, APRIL 25, 1910

CHAPTER XIV

Religious Teaching in Public Schools

ΙΕ IMPORTANCE OF a religious basis for education is at the present ɪme being widely recognized, and this is true whether we are thinking elementary schools or secondary schools or public schools. There ɪs always been a fear lest the religious teaching should be crowded ɪt, for when so much of a school curriculum has an examination in ɪew, a subject which does not pay in this respect is at a discount. ɪ regard to State controlled education—at the time of my writing ɪ do not know what final shape the Bill recently introduced by the ɪnister of Education will take—but the training of teachers, which vital in the whole matter, we hope will be definitely so arranged as ɪ include the power and the art of religious teaching, and will carry ɪeight in their preparation for their future careers.

It is a difficult thing to speak generally of the religious teaching our public schools. Many men consider that in this, as in many ɪepartments, things have stood still since they themselves were at ɪhool. I can recall after I became a Bishop a man distributing prizes ɪ a school who said to me before the ceremony began, "I fear I ɪall be saying things which you will not like." He went on to press ɪe importance of a better teaching of modern languages, but the forms which he advocated had already taken place during my own ɪreer as a schoolmaster. Moreover, the value of popular criticisms ɪ all the teaching in our public schools is also weakened by the fact ɪat many men are only acquainted with the particular masters and ɪssons with which they were personally concerned, and their general ɪquaintance with the questions involved is of too individual a ɪaracter, and too full of particular reminiscences, for them to make ɪy really serviceable contribution to the discussion of educational ɪforms.

I am not proposing to write a general essay on education nor on ɪligious education in particular, partly because the position in different ɪhools varies, and a proposal or scheme which would work well in ɪe school might be inappropriate in another. Everywhere, however, ɪ make religious education worthy of the name, the spiritual aspects ɪust be kept to the fore. However admirable and excellent may be ɪe traditional qualities exhibited by public school boys, good manners ɪd manner, the spirit of give and take, sportsmanship and gentle-ɪanly outlook, they do not carry us all the way to God, Who claims ɪyond and above these things our worship and our service and our

C

personal loyalty to Himself. What I intend to do is only this:
put down some of our ways and plans at Wellington College in ▨
time, giving a more or less accurate picture of the whole, but ▨
dreaming of suggesting that either in whole, or in part, it should ▨
imposed upon other schools.

It was my habit, after the first ten days of term had passed, ▨
gather together all the new boys in the Chapel: the ten days had, ▨
least, given them some slight idea of what the place would be li▨
and shown them something of the differences which contrasted ▨
on the one hand with their experiences at home, and on the otl▨
with the régime of their preparatory schools. I used to urge the
not to say or to do or to take part in anything which, when holid▨
came round, they would not be pleased to talk over with a favour▨
sister, saying how miserable it would make them when they return
home to have some secret experiences in their hearts to which they ho▨
that no kind of reference might be made in the home atmosphere.

I gave to them two little copies of a printed Bible reading sche▨
published for the benefit of schoolboys. I asked them to keep c▨
copy and to read the passage suggested for each day, day by day:
send the other copy home and to plan with their mother, perh▨
with other members of the family, that the same passage they w▨
reading at school would be read at home on the same day. There
certainly a fellowship in such Bible reading and it requires no apparat▨
only the possession of a Bible and the provision of a table of passag▨
I would perhaps tell them the story of a boy who came to be a gr▨
friend of mine who told me how miserable his first night at sch▨
had been, and then added: "My last night was sadder still, to th▨
that I was leaving a place where I had had so many happy year▨
Once a boy wrote to me who had left the school in disgrace and ▨
his letter said: "When I heard you tell that story I said to mys▨
'That shall be true of my last night.'" Poor boy, it was, but i▨
very different sense from what he had intended.

I used to feel that it was of great importance to keep the boys ▨
close touch with the best influences of home life, and I would dw▨
upon it, and I much respected the tears which would fill some ey▨
One of the school hymns contained the line: *Keep the spell of ho*
affection still alive in every heart. I often noticed that the gra▨
faults of boys revealed themselves towards the end of the term, wl▨
it was long since they had seen and been with those who made ▨
their home circle. I can remember a boy who had done someth▨
or other that was wrong and I wondered how it was that having g▨
as far as he had, he checked himself before taking the next and wo▨
step. He said to me quite simply: "I thought of my mother."

The Confirmation Day was a great day for the candidates, and the
paration for it was much more easily managed than it can be in a
ish. It was important that the preparation should grip the boys
their actual life. I used always to see the whole number of the
didates once a week, and speak to them all in a manner that
uld relate the Confirmation to their ordinary thoughts and sur-
ndings. At the end of each address I would give to the boys three
y easy and obvious questions upon what I had just said to them.
e answers they were to take to their tutors, who shared this happy
k with me. This little plan not only made the boys attentive,
wing that they would have to listen carefully and to put down
wers to some short and simple questions, but it also kept the tutors
me close together in the matter. Every year I would see in groups
the boys who had been previously confirmed one, two, and three
rs before; those of each year constituting the group: then there
e the older ones still, whom I would see together. Among all these
ked every boy who would like to come and see me again about his
firmation, to do so, and it was quite easy to arrange that he could
this without becoming conspicuous. I not only saw together all
candidates for the ensuing Confirmation week by week in the
pel, but I also had a personal interview with every boy, seeing
e of them twice over individually.

In these interviews I certainly did not encourage any personal
losures, and I would make it plain to any boy who began to tell
any of the unsatisfactory details of his school life that I should
regard what he said as confidential, and I would ask him to promise
he would not, whenever he met me, suppose that I was thinking
vhat he had said. Every year, when the Confirmation had taken
e, I asked the candidates in batches to come to tea in my house.
n the tea-table I summoned each one in turn and gave him a Prayer
k with his initials on it, and wrote his name in it. It has been
sant to find how much these books were treasured in after years.
When I look back upon my own Confirmation, it appears to me
ave been rather remote from the thoughts and difficulties and
ptations in the life of a growing boy at a school or at home. I
a to have vague recollections of very elementary Church history,
I carried away more about the landing of St. Augustine in England
the conflict against the world, the flesh, and the devil.

am generally in favour of boys being confirmed at school with
r fellows, for school life is the scene of their chief efforts, but I
ys urged a boy's mother or relations from home to be present.
makes a sacred association in the things of God, and builds up a
ed memory for the years to come. It is a great thing if school

and home can be united in the highest way. I was averse from b
coming to their public school already confirmed at home or at th
preparatory school before they have confronted the temptations
later boyhood and really understand what the service of God invol
Confirmation is not a magical protection, and requires a concurr
purpose.

There were so-called 'Divinity' lessons, always on Sunday
Monday, and sometimes also a lesson in the middle of the we
This mid-week lesson I would sometimes take myself, and it
an attraction to the boys that I did not deal with their own prepa
work, and anything that they had got ready could be carried forw
for the next lesson in the routine of the class. I found that the pa
set on 'Divinity' at the end of the term, when one master would be
off to examine the work done by the class of one of his colleag
tended to be of a very jejune style. If the class presented the
of the Apostles for the examination, the examiner would ask for a
of St. Paul's travels, and insert no question to elicit the fact that
candidates had been taught to regard the Book of the Acts as
Gospel of the Holy Spirit. So I used to place one or two question
a spiritual character into every 'Divinity' examination paper, ci
lating to the examiners the kind of answers that I was expecting
my questions.

In the winter of every year a retired missionary Bishop wc
visit us and speak to the whole number on a Sunday afternoon ab
his experiences in the mission field, and in thanking him for his kind
I would ask the boys, of whom many were sure to go to India
elsewhere in the Empire, to get into touch with the missionaries in
district. It is, I know, difficult to bring off such a plan; but s
sympathy, if it can be promoted between the missionaries and
Army officers or civil administrators, is very valuable. Someti
the missionary has, or thinks he has, no time to see anything of
lay neighbours, and the civilian does not give a thought to the ne
activities of the missionary. In the last thirty years no doubt n
is known and thought about missionary enterprise, and the Eng
Governors are much more inclined to regard the missionaries as
important colleagues in the work of administration, educat
and civilization. But the earlier we can induce boys to th
sympathetically of foreign missions so much the better.

When Easter fell very early we would spend it at school and
ten minutes before tea I would read in the Chapel some passages fr
a *Life of Christ*. Attendance was quite voluntary, but the num
who came made it well worth while. On Good Friday we we
have some kind of sacred concert, the performers being the b

mselves and not people from outside. On Easter Day all the
rs who were Communicants would be invited to come to the early
vice by way of a welcome to the newly confirmed, for our Con-
mation always took place just before Easter; and I would put some
ll Easter card, writing a word or two on it, in the place of every
r in the chapel to greet him for the Easter services.

It is often said that obligatory daily services reduce the interest
oys in going to church. A good deal may be said upon either side,
I doubt whether it is true that boys in a body revolt against the
ular services, and it is proper that for young people there should
a discipline of habit while they are too young to be left entirely
hoose for themselves. No doubt there will be grumbles, and boys
l be glad of a pretext for being excused attendance in Chapel. But
y would miss it if such services were taken from them. Without
ag able to put it into words they would, or many of them would, I
cy, be sorry if the attendance of the whole school were not expected
marking the spiritual foundation of their common life. But in
nning the style of worship we need a sense of proportion. We have
ee to it that, in a changing world, we do the best that is possible to
ag the worship and the service of God into the life of men and
nen and boys and girls.

In the Spring term coughing in the chapel was so frequent and
ontrolled as to make it difficult for the preacher to be heard.
the masters who were ordained used to preach by my invitation,
l I preached at irregular times: there was a sermon only in the
rning, and not in the evening, and we seldom had a preacher
n outside. In order to prevent boys who were anxious to listen
n being unable to hear, and indeed in the spirit of general reverence,
emember asking before the sermon all the boys who could not
trol their coughs to walk out of the Chapel and to sit in the Library.
re a prefect was ready to welcome them, and he had instructions
see that his little congregation remained with him in the Library
a quarter of an hour after the conclusion of the service in the
pel. My recollection is that his congregation was very much
uced on the second occasion; apparently I had hit upon a useful
tment for the curing of coughs.

Later on it may be well that young men should be left free to
ose, but anyone can notice that it is not really true of English
ple that they are wholly averse from Church services. Many of
m are glad to come on occasions of national or special or personal
ortance, and the way in which they attend on such an occasion
es it clear that the generality of ordinary people would feel a loss
hurch-going were altogether remote from their lives. Many motives

may combine in this respect, some conventional, some sentimen
some spiritual, but I like to think that when, after a long sile
the bells were rung after our victory in North Africa, there was s
general feeling that God had been with us and that in our wors
we could gratefully acknowledge His sovereignty over us and
nearness to us all.

Fewer headmasters are now ordained: more schools have spe
chaplains to conduct the services, to give 'Divinity' lessons, to prep
Confirmation candidates, etc. Probably the result of this is to th
the spiritual aspects of school life into a particular department a
to make the guidance of them more professional. The times cha
and I repeat, in conclusion, what I said at the beginning, that no
could be so foolish as to suppose that any departure from a rout
that worked well in days gone by marks a declension from the b

CHAPTER XV

Queen Victoria

IT WAS A red-letter occasion at Wellington when, on the day of
relief of Mafeking, Queen Victoria paid a visit to the College where
grandson, Lord Carisbrooke, then a small boy, was at school.

His mother, Princess Beatrice, accompanied the Queen, and
Duke of Connaught was also present. Even for this little and un
portant visit careful preparations were made beforehand by th
who were in attendance upon her. The whole number came
fourteen. For example, a small platform to reach from the door of
carriage to the entrance to the Master's Lodge was put in place,
that she might not have to step downwards, but would easily w
down on a sloping plane on the arm of her Indian supporter.
course it was necessary that this little plane should fit exactly
carriage door, and one of her suite had placed a little bit of pape
the bottom of the slope to indicate to the coachman precisely
point at which the wheel of the carriage must be brought to a stands
Her own coffee was sent over previously, and the chair was selec
on which she should sit. Her own wheel-chair was in readiness.
this she came across to the school buildings, visiting the Chapel and
Library. She read the terms of the award of the gold medal

nually presented to a boy chosen for the honour, calling the small
mpany to her side to tell a little story about it.

It was a private visit and, with the exception of Sir Lintorn
mmons, the Governors of the College were not present. The Queen
oke with him in her beautiful voice about the good news of the day.
fore she left the drawing-room, the Queen planted into a small
t, on a tray, a tiny sprig of fir which we later put out into the grounds.

When a suggestion was made that she should write her name in
e formal book before she left, those that were about her said that
would tire her less to write at Windsor and the book could be sent
ck. I possess a souvenir of her visit in an autograph letter from
er Majesty written a week before the visit came off; it is interesting
note that, though she had a lifelong experience of writing in the
rd person, she, like other people, found a difficulty in consistently
intaining that class of expression.

The boys were lined up on either side of the Rhododendron Avenue
ding up to the great gate of the College for her departure, and the
ad of the school presented a bouquet to Her Majesty, and the
ungest boy another to Princess Beatrice. The Queen had been with
e Prince Consort at the inauguration of the College many years
fore on what was then a lonely stretch of heather in a part of Windsor
rest. Now the district is built over in many directions, and it is
ply shown how wise it was at the beginning to secure four hundred
es for the grounds of the College, so that it should stand up the
re conspicuously as a memorial of the Great Duke.

This visit—paid in the last year of the Queen's long life and long
gn—will be remembered by all who shared in the honour of wel-
ning her. Wherever she went she was the impersonation of the
owing Empire, and evoked a romantic loyalty. She would not
ow herself for an afternoon without making it a great occasion.
e was above the common intercourse. When she appeared in public,
hearts were with her, and all eyes upon her. I do not know if she
s aware of the self-effacing humour of her remark after the great
bilee procession: "I saw nothing." But everyone who saw her felt
at they had caught a glimpse of something that was greatest and
epest in our history.

I venture to add the story of the laying of the foundation-stone
the College fifty years before, as told in a sermon I delivered in
e College Chapel on June 27th, 1901, after the Queen's death. In
I used the newspaper of the time.

*It was on Monday, June 2nd, 1856, that the Foundation Stone, which
u have seen in the front quadrangle, was laid by Her Majesty in person.*

The Queen in her reply said in words that conveyed the same tend
feeling that has inspired all her conduct during the course of this rece
War: "While gratefully admiring the gallantry and devotion which ha
been so conspicuously displayed by my army in the late War, I ha
deeply sympathized with the domestic sorrows and privations (the inevital
result of war) which have made so many mourners. I feel that we cann
better celebrate the re-establishment of peace than by laying the foundatic
of an institution which, while it will tend to soothe those sorrows ar
to mitigate the severity of those privations, will hold up to the imaginatie
of all those who share its benefits, the example of disinterested patriotis
of an unceasing devotion to his country's service, of an honesty of purpos
and of a determination in the performance of his duty, by which the lo
and brilliant career of the Duke of Wellington was so eminently disti
guished. I can express no better wish for my own son who bears the nan
of that great man, than that he should take as his guide through life t.
example of one with whom it will ever be his highest distinction to ha
been connected. I heartily join with you in commending this infa
institution to the divine blessing, and in praying that, with its increasi
prosperity, the benevolent intention of its Founders may be fully realized
"It would be quite superfluous," says the account, "to praise the distin
clearness of Her Majesty's voice. Every word, though uttered in a lo
tone, was clear and perfectly audible. Once and once only did her voi
waver, and it was at that portion of the reply which alluded in so touchi
a manner to the young Prince Arthur following as his guide and examp
the illustrious warrior whose godson he is."

CHAPTER XVI

Five Reigns

THE LITTLE STORY just given of Queen Victoria's visit to Wellingto
College at the end of her reign offers an opportunity for placing
record some personal observations upon the five sovereigns in who
reign I have lived, and with each of whom I have, in a greater or less
degree, come in contact.

It was Bishop Lightfoot, I believe, who made the oft-quoted remar
that the study of history is the best cordial for drooping spirits. Whe
we think of God's providence guiding the affairs of men, we are wise
consider it on a large scale. This is not to rule out the conception th
in the smaller affairs of personal life God's finger may be seen to be

ork by those who live close to Him. But however real their belief
ay be that God directs the details of the events among which they
ove, this kind of trust cannot carry conviction to others at second
and. It is in the larger issues of life, extending over a considerable
ne and area, that we can together believe in God as supreme in the
fairs of men. When in the Creed we express our faith in God Almighty
e have to remember that we are not speaking of God as able to do
erything and anything, the Greek equivalent word shows Him to
as holding an exercised sovereignty.

This is brought home to us as we consider the reigns in England
the last hundred years. We can well believe that God gave to our
untry and empire the right sovereign at the right moment, the one
ho was personally fitted to meet the changing needs of each period.
would be necessary to write a history of the last century and five
ll biographies if a survey of all the relevant considerations were
ndertaken. But in these little reflections we can only look at the
rsonalities concerned and at their correspondence with the place
ey were called to fill.

The Monarchy had fallen low after the reign of George III. What-
er we may think of him as a king we can have little admiration
r his sons. His own contemporaries thought poorly of William IV.
mportant events happened in his reign and he met the occasions
tter than might have been expected from one who was lacking in
rsonal ability. If he had been succeeded by a brother the Monarchy
ould have fallen irretrievably. At this juncture it was retrieved
d reformed by the ascent to the throne by a young girl who
cessarily brought with her a touch of romance.

She had a fine conception of her position as a constitutional
vereign, and through her long reign she built up a tradition which
as largely due to her character and capacity and to the loyalty that
e evoked. By the end of her reign she had become the impersonation
English history, of the expansion of England, and of the growth
an Empire. Her judgment was unchallenged, and without over-
epping the mark she was able to put her hand on public affairs
th firmness, prudence, and insight. She was fortunate in her
arriage, and learnt much from association with her husband.
lthough during his lifetime he remained largely unappreciated, yet
the years have gone by his worth has been more and more fully
cognized. People may still smile at some of his un-English habits;
t his sagacity, his foresight, and his devotion to the cause of his
lopted country are accepted facts. In recent years the greatness of
e Queen and the way in which she bridged the gap between the past
d present régime has won general approval and applause.

c*

She spoke of herself as having almost become a legendary figu
in her lifetime, and those who knew her only towards the end of l
reign need an effort of imagination to picture what England was li
sixty years before—those sixty years had included much. Thou
she did not initiate or stand behind all the advances made, she wa
for example, rather strangely independent of the way in which wom
came to the front yet, everyone felt the strength and stability th
arose from the fact that she was there, and that she gave a coheren
to the developments which marked her epoch at home and abroa
When she died, at the beginning of this century, it seemed as if t
landmarks had been moved and as if the career of England could n
be the same without her. After her jubilee in 1887 the concludi
years of her life had a halo over them: she came more into pub
prominence, and the aloofness which through many years had chara
terized her mourning for the Prince Consort seemed to melt awa

When she died it was thought that an impossible task devolv
upon her successor. But the right man took her place. His abili
at the time had so far by no means been appreciated. His father h
not brought him up as an ordinary English boy, sharing in the l
of his contemporaries, and his mother had granted him no responsibili
to develop his capacities. She not only overshadowed him, b
accustomed to dictate and to assert her will, she kept him in an utter
subordinate place.

It has been said of men in public life that one of the first dut
of the holder of an office is to train his successor, but this is not alwa
recognized in more personal relations. You will often find a m
who appears to be jealous of his heir. I think of a squire with a lar
and important property who used constantly to complain that l
predecessor had altogether refused to talk over with him the respon
bilities which would one day fall to him. He would speak bitte
of the treatment to which he had been subjected, and all the tir
he was treating his own eldest son in the same way! One of the fine
things in the character of King Edward VII was the uncomplaini
and loyal patience with which he was prepared to be misjudged a
thought to be chiefly interested in unimportant things. Natural
there were ways and methods in his mother's outlook which had last
quite long enough and changes were required. The glorious reign
Queen Victoria needed to be modernized. When his turn came,
achieved this in the most human of ways.

The Queen's absences in Scotland had imposed a strain upon l
ministers, and in some of her ways there was a vein of tyranny. Tru
feminine to the end, she was really pleased when, in her old age la
one night, a sentry at Windsor Castle, seeing a light burning in l

ndow and little thinking whose room it was, called out: "Good ght, Miss."

Memorial services, and other things dear to the heart of the Queen, re discontinued; establishments at Royal Palaces were reduced; thful retainers were wisely pensioned off. In all the great things of e King Edward fulfilled the promise of his first speech that so long he lived he would devote himself to his country's welfare. Indeed did.

In an important book, recently written by Lord Ponsonby, dealing th the work of his father, Queen Victoria's Private Secretary, con-lerable notice is taken of attempts taken to find some appropriate here in which the Prince of Wales, as he then was, could fulfil his otto. It proved difficult to reach any suitable solution.

Moreover, some have considered that later on, when he came to e throne, there was nothing behind his apparent success: It was e, so they would say, not to any real ability that he possessed, but his geniality, social gifts, and good-heartedness which captivated d misled those who supposed that his ready insight came from real owledge. Such critics would maintain that as a matter of fact he d not ever master a subject with care and diligence and concentrated tention.

It is true that he was not a great reader, except of newspapers; t he could quickly read men, and it seems doubtful whether anyone, wever quick in the uptake, could disguise from so many eyes a nt of natural capacity, and pass for a great man when he was really allow and not a genuine and thoughtful leader.

The unfavourable characterizations may have been more or less urate in early times, but there is a grace of office, as Bishop Westcott uld call it, and in commoner language we indicate such an idea en we say of one and another that, when his time came, he rose to occasion. Perhaps it was true of the Emperor Augustus.

The short reign of King Edward marked a definite transition m the old ways of Queen Victoria's régime to the more modern rld which was then arising before the eyes of men. It may be ing an injustice to the King to judge him against the background the estimates and views of the Queen and those on whom she ied. "Other times: other men." It is right to mention these two inions of him; possibly the truth may lie somewhere between them. lo not presume to suggest at what point any such change, if change re was, might have come or been developed. When the King's rk was accomplished he was acclaimed a wonderful king. He d matched the progress of his time. When he died there was a iversal sense of bereavement which only revealed itself as the days

went by; but one and another and yet another in conversation ga
his opinion of the King, and this swelled into a chorus of person
mourning in which everyone felt that he had lost a friend of his ow
even the failings of the King had endeared him; for in a fresh way
had welded together the new elements appearing in our public li

Some called him Edward the Peacemaker. At home and abro
he justified this title. As a matter of fact it belonged to him fro
his very birth. There had been friction between the masters and t
boys at Eton; defiance on the one side was not cured by punishme
on the other, but when news came on November the ninth that
heir had been born to the throne of England, the wise Headmas
declared that the dispute could continue no longer, and they all settl
down again in contentment and peace. The little child was born
Prince of peace.

King George used to say that he had no training in the art
kingship. He was the second son of his father and looked for
elder brother to succeed to the throne. He was brought up for t
Navy, in which he gained a good knowledge of the Empire and oth
lands. It was the Navy which trained his outlook, and so far as
had any philosophy of life the Navy gave it to him; it taught him
judge by results and constantly to put the practical question: "H
is the proposal to be carried out, and how will it work?" Fr
long intercourse with all kinds of people he gained a practical shrev
ness; when asked on an occasion what could reunite some promine
men who could help the country if, after a recent political disagr
ment, they should come together again and co-operate, he replie
"Time, time, time"—not of course a deep remark, but revealing a sou
acquaintance with human nature. It was this absence of spec
training which made him the remarkable King that he became a
gave to him a universal appeal.

There was an artificiality in the education which the father
Edward VII imposed on his son; pictures and books were to be
about to lead the young Prince to ask questions: but King Geo
was to be reared like other English boys. This was exactly what
needed for his career. The ten years of his father's reign had carr
the world still farther from Queen Victoria, and however skilf
King Edward had met or created the new atmosphere, there w
still certain restrictions upon the King in dealing with every sort
kind of persons on an equality of footing. These, so far as was ri
King George removed. He was not a man with political insight
his father. He had no theories to back up. He was one who w
simplicity and friendliness came near to others without condescens
They could understand him, and they felt that he could underst

em. .There was at times something winning in his very artlessness:
nen he was Prince of Wales a big Church appointment had just been
ade; he turned to me and exclaimed: "Have you seen the announce-
ent? What *do* you think of choosing such a man? I'm not going
say a *word*, I'm only asking what *you* think?" He could work
th various sorts of people happily and successfully, and if he was
home with the members of different governments he could also
ter into the ordinary ways of ordinary folk. He was confronted
th troublous times from the beginning of his career, and he said to
e that the outbreak of the European War gave him a positive relief
om the difficulties of the situation at home and in Ireland. His
dustry was great, and if papers were circulated before a meeting he
ould have mastered them. He was punctual, putting his work first,
d attending assiduously to the pile of red boxes. It is very exacting
nstantly to be turning from one interview to another, from one
bject to something altogether different.

When he had gone to Scotland for a holiday he returned almost the
xt day on his spontaneous initiative when the Government of that
ne had to face a financial crisis. He read his Bible regularly, and his
mestic life set a standard for all. Through everything he had the
onderful help and companionship of Queen Mary.

Before the end of his life he had learnt how his people loved him,
at the beginning of his reign neither he nor the Queen were fully
own. The War brought them out and made their power of sympathy
be seen and applauded. The country and the Empire by this time
eded a king whom the common man could understand, and the
mmon man felt that the King belonged to him.

There was a change when Edward VIII took his father's place.
e was a man of a different style, and was out of sympathy with the
andards of kingship as worked out in the previous three reigns. There
as a singular charm about him when he was young, and this never
t him. He possessed, like a poet, the art of interpreting and expres-
ng for them the thoughts which lay deep down in the hearts of many.
ut he adopted, as time went on, an independence of behaviour, and
as impatient of guidance, lacking the self-control which is demanded
those in high positions if they are to conform to what is expected
them and to carry through plans previously set out. It may be
at his best work had already been achieved when he went from
untry to country as an ambassador of Empire. It was a very hard
d continuous occupation for him, and the Government of the day
ver spared him, but kept him on the move. He had few spells of
iet home life, and was wanting in the calmness and composure
ich they might have brought him to check the restlessness of his

disposition. If the view just expressed that he had fulfilled the mot
of the Prince of Wales—translated, 'I serve'—before his father's dea
is correct, then we can see that it is really appropriate that he shou
never be crowned as king, but God had used his gifts in earlier yea
The last of his services was by comparison to make an indire
preparation for his brother's reign.

We now have a King and a Queen who meet splendidly the requi
ments of these exacting times. The King has expanded since he ca
to the throne, and his indefatigable war efforts have won gold
opinions. Queen Elizabeth has always been at his side. He has be
identified with every phase of the war endeavour and is constant
among the men and women serving their country at sea, on land, a
in the air, and among those who are working on the home front. It
marvellous that he can carry on his regular work as King, for it nev
ceases, and yet be ubiquitous in travelling over the country.
all recognize the fine manner in which he rises to every occasion. T
War has been as hard on him as upon his people. He knows wh
war bereavement is, for just when the plans were being made to fu
his desire for a weekday to be spent by the nation in prayer a
dedication, he was himself called upon to mourn for the loss of
beloved brother.

From his coronation day onwards he has captured the hearts
all, and has led them along a straight course of devotion and se
dedication. He and the Queen have not called from a distance up
others to dare and to bear; they have first given themselves, and
giving have exhibited unobtrusively a high standard of confiden
courage, and godliness. We echo the words of the Book of Proverl
'The throne is established by righteousness.'

With thankful hearts we can conclude this little review of Go
never-failing providence in what He has in recent years done
England by quoting Cowper's uplifting words:

> *Deep in unfathomable mines*
> *Of never failing skill,*
> *He treasures up His bright designs*
> *And works His sovereign will.*

CHAPTER XVII

My Episcopate

WAS CONSECRATED Bishop of Norwich in St. Paul's on April 25th,
10. I was presented to Archbishop Davidson by Francis Paget,
shop of Oxford—a dear friend of mine with whom I often stayed
Cuddesdon (I was working at the time in his diocese)—and by John
ordsworth, Bishop of Salisbury, who had ordained me deacon and
iest. This could not have happened unless both of us had become
shops rather early in life. The sermon was preached by Dr. Butler,
en Master of Trinity College, Cambridge, to whom I had often
rned in my schoolmaster days, though when I was myself at Trinity
was not yet Master. When first I was nominated I was invited by
chbishop Davidson to come and see him, and he urged me not to
distressed by the fact that I had never worked in a parish, quoting
ustrations to prove his point; but he added: "At the moment
ere are many items familiar to a rural dean with which you are
acquainted."

I felt the necessity of making every possible use of such experience
ssessed by the rural deans. Eager not to impose upon the clergy
a rural deanery anybody of my own choice without consulting their
shes, I made and always followed a scheme of asking every clergyman
send to me through the archdeacon three names of his own choice
r the office, in the order of his preference, from which, after adding
and scrutinizing the votes, I could choose the right man.

Later I adopted the plan of commissioning a new rural dean in
blic in his own church with his brethren present, together with the
ngregation of the parish, explaining the little-understood nature of
e office and my own reliance upon the help of the rural deans. Often
turned to them for advice on parochial matters in the deanery:
ey could put for me any item which might have reached me into its
oper place and proportion, for it is a mistake for a bishop to deal
ith every question. This would tend to exaggerate trifles, or bring
em into formal investigation. The archdeacon is always at hand to
lp, and often the rural dean can give a friendly word of counsel
the clergyman of a parish so that a small point may be settled in it.
vice a year, like most bishops, I invited to my house all the arch-
acons and rural deans, and I would then put before them matters
which I needed their guidance.

When I went into the diocese as bishop it contained about a
ousand parishes. It comprised all Norfolk and East Suffolk. A

hundred years before it had included the western side of Suffolk a
well. Plans were already developed for the division of the dioces
It was not a very satisfactory scheme, for it was to constitute fiv
dioceses out of three. County feeling is strong and constantly helpfu
But this scheme ran counter to it, for it transferred a part of Norfo
into the Ely diocese, and kept a part of Suffolk in the diocese
Norwich, which, in the end, was reduced by some three hundre
parishes. Two of these parishes were in many cases united togethe
so that the number of parishes was greater than the number of clerg
and the plan for such unions has been simplified and gone on apa
since then. The division was finally effected after I had been Bish
of Norwich for three or four years. The Great War, beginning abo
the same time, prevented me from assessing accurately the differenc
it made in the work, and I was already finding that, moving abo
in a motor, I was able on one Sunday to accomplish what would ha
taken my predecessors one or two week-end visits to achieve.

When there were many fewer bishops than there are now it w
the habit of the bishops of East Anglia to spend two nights in t
autumn in the house of one of themselves in rotation. They we
accompanied by their wives, who held meetings of their own whi
their husbands were discussing matters of common interest. Tim
was found for walks in the afternoon and there was a reception in t
evening for people who lived near. When my turn arrived I had
considerable dinner-party. These gatherings were very agreeable
the days when bishops attended fewer meetings in London.

The diocese of Norwich was, and is, a kind of miniature of t
Church of England as a whole. It has its large towns, its countr
towns, its seafaring folk and interests, and its many country village
which in some parts, in spite of improved transport, are still lonel
It is wonderful the way in which the rural clergy, to whom their peop
turn for help in every conceivable little puzzle, are in so many cas
the friends of their flocks. And who could adequately praise the
wives? It is no doubt true that many of these follow the fashion
the time and, putting first their own tastes and enjoyable outlet
have less inclination to foster the wholesome life of a small communit
but speaking generally we should be nowhere if we had not the syn
pathetic self-sacrifice of the wives of the clergy, and of their devot
daughters.

Norwich, once the second town in England, is the unquestion
capital of East Anglia, and I soon came to see that I was a citizen
no mean city, and had entered on a great heritage. In many way
Norfolk is apart from the rest of England. It has looked over the wat
for its enemies, for its trade, its architecture. Norwich has prosper

ecause it has adapted itself to changing requirements and its industries
ave developed accordingly. The people of Norfolk, high and low,
ve the very soil of the county and are independent of external
fluences, on which their back is turned literally and often
etaphorically.

I have read that the Bishops of Norwich have always occupied
ther an independent ecclesiastical position. They are still the
bbots of St. Benet. In the days of Henry VIII the See of Norwich
ll vacant, and the Abbot of St. Benet's mentioned to the King
at if he appointed him to the bishopric he would cede its valuable
nds at Lynn to the King and be content with the lands of the Abbey;
e ruins of which can be seen at Ludham to this day. The King
cted accordingly and the property of the See is still mainly in the
cinity of the Abbey.

CHAPTER XVIII

A Bishop's Office

WAS BISHOP OF NORWICH for three-quarters of the years of this
entury which have so far gone by. I have seen changes come over a
ishop's work of which I will write more fully when I give some account
f my time in Norwich. But there are some misconceptions about the
ork of a bishop which are still prevalent. There are those who
hink of a bishop as one who holds a leisurely, dignified office and is
lentified with the aristocracy. About half of the bishops have seats
a the House of Lords, and this fact fosters the misapprehension: a
ishop is often seen at public ceremonials and his utterances are
onstantly reported. In years gone by, in previous generations, there
hay have been more to justify such an estimate. We can think of a
Velsh bishop who never set foot in his diocese, and devoted himself to
mprovements in the Lake District. But a great change has taken
place in the whole body of bishops since those days of long ago. It
s the work that is not seen or done in public which takes up the
reater part of a bishop's time. One might almost say that his occupa-
ions are primarily administrative. This no doubt would be going too
ar, for after all it is the spiritual aspects of his work which count for
nost. Every bishop spends much of his time, for instance, over his
rdinations and confirmations. A hundred years ago a bishop would

only hold confirmations once in three years, and then hundreds and hundreds of male and female candidates would be assembled at large centres, some spending the night there with inevitable risks. Now it is the habit of bishops to confirm either in single parishes or in smaller areas, and this they will do every year on some more or less fixed routine, sharing the duty with the assistant bishops whom they have to help them. But no account of this work reaches further than the local Press.

Then it falls to the bishop to institute, either in church or privately at his house, every new incumbent of a benefice. When the bishop has instituted the new incumbent the archdeacon inducts him, and it is curious to notice how frequently the institution and induction are confused in the Press and in common parlance. This is an evidence of the commonly scant acquaintance with a bishop's work. Every bishop has a number of benefices, smaller or larger, in his own gift, and it is for him to choose the right man to fill every one of these. The patron of a benefice has the right and the duty to present a clergyman to fill a vacancy that has arisen by the death or the removal of the existing incumbent, as he is called, who has held the particular benefice. If the patron has not presented within six months of the vacancy occurring, the presentation lapses to the bishop. After another six months it lapses to the Archbishop of the province, and finally after another six months the lapse falls to the Crown. Now it can easily be imagined that if a diocese comprises three, four, or five hundred parishes, even when two parishes are united to constitute one benefice, the amount of correspondence involved is very large. Frequently in the case of livings which offer no adequate stipend the patron will write to the bishop at the beginning and ask him to find a suitable man.

Another task of the bishop is to examine and ordain candidates for the Ministry and to find for each man who is ordained a suitable sphere of work in a curacy. Some bishops may do more than others in regard to the share which they take in the examination, though the greater part of the work falls to their examining chaplains. (When the time for an ordination comes round the bishop will give his whole attention to the candidates to make the time as profitable as possible for them and to send each new curate to his post with all the help that can be put within his reach.)

Then we must add the many complaints which bishops receive from parishes that have, or suppose they have, clergymen inadequate to their duties, and in this respect quite a small parish may give as much trouble in the matter of correspondence and enquiry as one with a larger population. A bishop's secretary is a busy man or woman.

nd to be a bishop's chaplain, to help him in all this work, is no sinecure. But of all this work the public hears very little. There may be plenty f talk in the particular parish, but it is not of sufficient interest to he world at large for anything to be said about it outside.

Every bishop possesses a Chancellor and a Diocesan Registrar, oth of whom help with the legal aspects of his work, and in an stablished church such points may frequently arise for discussion, nd in the rare cases of clergy who have neglected their duties or rought discredit upon their office the bishop may be involved in eally intricate proceedings which take up much of his time and hought.

It will be seen then how much of a bishop's time is spent in lay-to-day occupations, for many of the matters which I have lescribed involve interviews and correspondence and second and third nterviews. No bishop can ever tell what the post will bring him. Ie cannot tell who will be writing to him or the subject upon which he letters will be written. The mysterious atmosphere which hangs bout a bishop leads some to suppose that he possesses an unlimited uthority and can put everything right if he will take appropriate ction. They little know how his powers are circumscribed even in natters which may rightly be thought to fall within his province. Ie is anything but an autocrat. He is under the authority of the Law, and the clergy can create opposition. Suasion, not coercion, nust be his usual line of action.

If a bishop is to keep abreast with his work he will be wise to avoid an accumulation of arrears. Some bishops frequently say how busy they are; many people work quite as hard. The special feature, however, about bishops' work is that so much of it comes to them hrough the post and this they cannot regulate. But no man commends his occupations by constantly referring to them. It is better o get on with what has to be done than to talk about it. Habits and methods vary, and I once heard Archbishop Davidson say that he never put a notice in the paper asking to be spared correspondence when he was away from home. Some follow his example; others do not. I can remember calling upon a bishop on the evening when he had returned from his holiday; perhaps it was inconsiderate to go to see an old friend even for a few minutes. He happened to remark to me that he had on that day written seventy letters.

Enough has been said to indicate that a bishop's is a hard office demanding industry, concentration, and discrimination in the things he does himself and those which he is ready to depute. Certainly, considering all the expense involved in keeping up an expensive palace with an adequate staff, it is plain that a bishop does not belong

to the opulent classes. It is not then very clear why there is so muc
misapprehension with reference to a bishop's position or why he :
considered as a suitable figure for small and foolish stories and satire
Perhaps a bishop's official dress has something to do with this. Ther
are some who consider that it is a pity that bishops and archdeacor
wear breeches and gaiters, and also that the parochial clergy have
dress of their own. In some respects these habits are being modifiec
and I believe I must be about the last bishop who always wears th
large bishop's hat as was usual in former days. Thirty years se
changes.

CHAPTER XIX

Deans of Norwich

I HAVE OFTEN in a humorous spirit remarked that I served 'under
four Deans. It had seemed to me—for some years before I became
bishop—that it was very sad to observe the manner in which bishop
and deans were prone to get at variance with one another. I mad
up my mind that I would never quarrel with a dean, even if I wa
convinced that in some matter he was wrong and I was right
Probably one of the reasons of such friction arises from the fact tha
a bishop and a dean and chapter are in most cases capable men, an
live very near to one another: the dean and chapter, though havin
plenty of work on hand, have the ability and can find time fo
criticism of one another and of the bishop. A similar tendency t
mutual criticism is found in a body of schoolmasters living togethe
in a common room.

I can look back upon the Deans of Norwich whom I have known
and am grateful for much in my association with them. When
came to Norwich, the dean was Dr. Russell Wakefield, who succeede
Lefroy. Lefroy was famous as a preacher and died in his belovec
Switzerland. Dr. Russell Wakefield had not been there very lon
and stayed but a short time. In London he had been Rector o
St. Mary, Bryanston Square. He had interested himself in socia
questions, and had been Chairman of the Central Committee on th
Unemployed, President of the National Council of Public Morals, anc
a member of a Royal Commission on the Poor Law and of the Londor
School Board. At one time he was Mayor of Marylebone. He had
been educated in England, France and Germany, and was not only

n ecclesiastical figure. The intercourse of London life suited him
ell, and prominent people would come to stay with him in Norwich.
Ie was an authority on church appointments, and he carried weight
vith the ecclesiastical secretary in Downing Street. He had a friendly
1anner and a sunny smile, and both of these carried him far, though
here was not always power or resourcefulness behind them. His
.elicate wife counted for much in his home circle. When I had been
ne year in Norwich he was carried away to succeed Dr. Gore as
3ishop of Birmingham. He was fond of Norwich, and I used after-
vards to see him there as well as at meetings of bishops in London.
Ie was scarcely long enough in Norwich to make any great impression.

His successor also came to us from London, but they did not
esemble one another. Dr. Beeching was a Canon of Westminster,
.nd was marked by the Westminster tradition and outlook. He was
>recise in his views, and he disapproved of episcopal functions taking
>lace in the cathedral church; other deans liked me to institute
10norary canons in the cathedral before their installation there by
he dean. But deferring to the judgment of Dr. Beeching, during
1is period of office, I used to carry through these institutions previously.
5o, too, with ordinations; for the Trinity Ordination collided with the
Dedication Festival of the cathedral church, and I took to ordaining
n the large chapel of the Palace. Dr. Beeching was a fastidious
scholar who published sermons, poems and lectures on literary and
loctrinal subjects and produced editions of Milton and other English
poetical works.

He was pre-eminent for his taste, and it was a privilege to hear
1im reading the Lesson: his rendering of the Second Lesson on
Christmas morning is something to remember. He found a congenial
friend in Canon Westcott—whom I appointed Archdeacon of Norwich
—and they collaborated in a translation of the Epistle to the Hebrews.
Canon Westcott, like his father, was a senior classic in his Cambridge
tripos, and was headmaster of Sherborne before he accepted a resi-
lentiary canonry at Norwich. The statutes of the cathedral have
been revised since Beeching's days and points have been clarified,
notably in connection with the appointment of preachers. It fell to
Dr. Beeching to choose a vicar for Yarmouth in succession to Canon
Willink, and he showed his good sense in learning from Downing
Street who were the coming men, with the result that he selected the
Rev. C. Lisle Carr, then Rector of Woolton, Liverpool, who later
became Bishop of Coventry and afterwards Bishop of Hereford.

I first met Dr. Willink when he was Vicar of Great Yarmouth.
On the day after King Edward VII died I was to give away the prizes
at the Yarmouth Boys' School. I was not yet actually in residence

at the Palace, where much work was going on, but staying in th
western side of the county. I thought on the day that I ought t
visit Yarmouth and see what was being done. I invited myself t
lunch with Canon Willink, whom I found genial and welcoming
That was the way in which our friendship began. I did not see much
of him when he left Yarmouth for Birmingham, but greeted him as a
old friend when he came back to Norwich as dean. Once more we
had a dean of quite a different type. On the one hand he was ready
to go about and help the archdeacons in their work of inductions, etc.
and on the other he made the very most of the cathedral both for the
benefit of Norwich and over a wider area for confirmations and so on
He knew the families living in the extensive Close in Norwich and
with his large heart ministered to them. The service on Sunday
evenings in the nave appealed to him very much, and he made i
appeal very cordially to the many who frequented it. He preached
at the services, and with a strong body of nave stewards made that
evening service a real power in the life of the community. He
provided forms for the service and a special hymn book; the procession
at the beginning was a considerable feature. His experience at
Yarmouth and Birmingham tended to create a kind of parochial
feeling and an enthusiasm for the cathedral as if it were a great parish
church, and the throbbing centre of its life. He always came to my
meetings of the archdeacons with the rural deans, and his large
acquaintance with church life in Yarmouth made his presence helpful.
I remember him one day telling us that the circulation of the parish
magazine was enhanced when it contained portraits of prominent
parishioners. He had in many ways made Yarmouth, with its several
churches, one, under his leadership, and he brought the same spirit
into Norwich.

After the sudden death of Willink, Dr. Cranage succeeded him.
Once more we had a new style of dean, who already cared for every
stone in our lovely cathedral, less well known than it deserves to be;
but Norwich is not a city people pass through on their way elsewhere.
There is a combined strength and grace in the architecture of rare
beauty. The Dean in peace time used to lecture twice on the summer
Bank Holidays to the visitors who crowded in from our sea-coast
resorts. His knowledge of ecclesiastical and other architecture is
superb, and large sums of money have been spent not in restoration
but in revealing the beauties of this great fane. Recently the splendid
cloisters have received attention and the freshness of the colourful
details exposed. The Dean has written on church and monastic
architecture and life. Antiquarian and educational authorities,
councils for the Fine Arts and for the care of churches have turned to

im for help and advice. He is the Prolocutor of the Lower House
f Convocation of Canterbury. The baldest record of his services to
he Church of England as a whole, to Cambridge studies and ot
Norwich in particular reveals his distinction in public life, in which
ie bears himself with dignity, considerateness, calmness and a due
ense of proportion, with a manner which conciliates others and leads
o trust and confidence. But chiefly do I like to think with gratitude
f his never-failing goodness to me, and of all our brotherly association
ogether.

This little record of the deans I have known suggests the manifold
vay in which God can be, and is, served. To the list may be added
he name of Goulburn, who, before my time, was a great and acceptable
riter of widely read devotional books. There are diversities of gifts
ut the same spirit, and there are differences of administration but
he same Lord. A deanery offers a rich scope for such variety. There
s a fixed routine of work but, apart from that, a dean can choose his
irther activities; something of the same kind may be said of the
arochial clergy. Here is a noble part of the comprehensiveness of
he Church of England.

I must add an expression of my thankfulness to the body of
rchdeacons who have worked with me, and given fine service to the
iocese. They have been many.

CHAPTER XX

The Coronation

HREE CORONATIONS COME within my memory. I recall most vividly
he sadness of the postponement of King Edward's Coronation, owing
o his serious illness. The boys of Wellington College were to be
cattered in all directions in and near London to see the Procession,
nd the plans had been completed. But just before the day came for
hem to start, the distressing news reached me, and I collected the
oys from the playing-fields in their hundreds; using the new cricket
avilion for the first time. I announced that everything was cancelled;
ve then said the prayer for the King's Majesty.

I was in Westminster Abbey for the Coronation of King George V
nd Queen Mary. There were great crowds in the streets; but this
vas nothing like the concourse from all over England and the Empire

and, indeed, the world, which collected for the Coronation of Kin
George and Queen Elizabeth. What would have happened th
time if the buses had been running in Westminster? In 1911 it wa
quite possible to walk along Victoria Street in robes. The servic
in 1911 was longer than on the last occasion, when it was wisel
abbreviated without its salient and essential features being altere

We are apt to speak as if the crowning of the King was the mo
important item. It is no doubt the climax of the ceremony, and wh
that saw it would ever forget the beautiful sight of the peeresses a
all together, they raised their arms to put their own coronets on the
heads just as the King was being crowned by the Archbishop. Bu
on the spiritual side it is the anointing which is the focus of the servic
The Sovereign leaves the Abbey as the crowned King in the eyes
men; but before God he leaves as the Lord's Anointed.

I was present in the House of Lords when King Edward the Eight
addressed the Lords and the Commons at the Opening of Parliamen
which fell before the date arranged for his coronation; between tho
two dates—on November 10th—he abdicated. The coronation too
place on the date originally fixed—May 12th, 1939—but George V
was crowned instead of his brother. It was, from many points
view, wise to adhere to this date, towards which all the plans a
home and abroad had already been working. (Many difficultie
even law-suits, arose when the date of the Coronation of Edward V
was postponed.)

On the occasion of our present King's Coronation, the Clerk
the Closet being unwell, I was invited as the senior bishop, to whom
no function was allotted, to carry the Bible in the Procession. Th
involved attendance at some of the rehearsals, and no one could spea
too highly of the careful preparations made by the Archbishop
Canterbury so that there should be no jarring note or confusion, an
that everyone should know his part and be in the right place. Th
Duke of Norfolk, as Earl Marshal, was responsible for the conduct
the ceremony, and his quiet manner was beyond all praise: no fuss, i
agitation, perfect good humour and readiness to help everybod
The work accomplished by him and his staff through many weel
beforehand, and at the time of the rehearsals, was amazing. I ca
recall the interest he took in the actual Bible I was to carry. It wa
provided by the Oxford University Press, which made a noble effo
to mark the unique occasion. But the volume sent was too lar
and too heavy to be carried or manipulated, and it became necessar
to use a smaller Book.

In the Annexe, which was constructed at the West End of th
Abbey, everything was orderly, and on the day itself the vario

.icles to be used in the service were in their right places. The
lice regulations made it necessary that everyone should reach the
nexe some hours before the service began. By the goodness of
. Hannah, the Secretary, I was allowed, with my little girl and her
verness, to use two of the rooms in the office of Queen Anne's
ounty as bedrooms, and as this is in Dean's Yard, near the entrance,
was only a step across to the Abbey.

Time passed quickly and pleasantly; different people and groups
me in and passed through to their allotted places; there was a spirit
happy friendliness, and suppressed excitement on all sides. We
d been well drilled to do our bit at the correct moment. The
obey looked magnificent in gold and blue tapestry; a fit setting
the impressive pageantry of the scene. Others have described the
mbined effect of pomp and ceremony. My own seat was on one
the sedilia at the far east. Owing to a tendency to phlebitis, I was
t anxious to stand throughout the service, and I slipped through
small door which led into Henry VII's Chapel where I could sit and
st for a short time. This fine chapel was outside the whole function,
d had been thoughtfully equipped and staffed by the Red Cross as
first-aid post. (Having no patients on whom to lavish attentions,
ey were delighted to give me something more solid; and, after the
ry long morning, I was ready for a sandwich. Other people did
t fare so well, and some went without food for as long as ten hours.)
soon returned to my place in the service, which put me opposite
e pew in which, on a higher level, members of the Royal Family
ere gathered. The spectacle of uniforms and bishops' copes was
ry fine. I was wearing one especially beautiful, which had been
esented to the Cathedral Church of Norwich for the Bishop
Mr. J. Birkbeck in the year when he was High Sheriff of
orfolk.

The service did not prove so very long after all: there was no
rmon. The music was of a very high order, and beautifully rendered.
ie Westminster Boys did their traditional part in calling out,
ivat" at the exact moment. The Bishops who were concerned with
e special acts in the service, all gathered together behind the Arch-
shop as each trophy or treasure was presented to the King. (The
ean of Westminster, Dr. Foxley Norris, a few days afterwards sent
e some of the wool with which the King had been anointed. I have
still. It was a tiring day for the Dean, who had to be on his legs
roughout, and it proved too much for him.)

The Bible is presented to the King after he has been crowned:
her trophies are put into his hand beforehand. Memorable words
e used by the Archbishop when he hands the Bible. It is called

the most valuable thing that this world affords: "Here is wisdom this is the royal law: these are the lively oracles of God."

I was one of the very few people who, being beyond them to the east, could clearly see the full faces of the King and Queen. Wherever one looked it was a scene of splendour and beauty, such as no other country could gather together at the present time, and one felt that all that was great and grand in our English tradition—right through the centuries—was nobly preserved and here represented. But it was the faces of the King and Queen against this wonderful background of grace and glory that I shall always dwell upon with delight. There was a look of sincerest devotion on their countenances, and I found myself whispering: "God is very near and they know it."

One must throw one's mind back a few years to realize how the King and Queen, after the Coronation, and after the King's broadcast that evening, had won all hearts. We know this so well now that it needs a little effort to remember that previously the King had played a minor part in public affairs, and, after the agitations of the previous reign, he had made his own way into the hearts of his subjects. It was felt all over the world that nothing like the Coronation could have taken place elsewhere, and that no parallel to this consecration of the life of the nation and the empire, as represented by the King's own anointing and Coronation, could be found. He, indeed, stood for his people; and his people soon came to know that he was worthy to do so.

It is not now necessary to speak of the end of the service, or of the trying but pardonable confusion which arose in the calling of motors in the pouring rain. It was simply impossible for the owner of a car to be on the pavement at the very moment when his car reached the appointed spot; several unfortunate ladies fainted from exhaustion and lack of food. Personally I had nothing to complain of, and found myself soon taking tea with my family in the Governors' room in Queen Anne's Bounty before returning to the place where I was staying.

The glory and beauty of holiness which adorned the Abbey has left a lasting impression on my mind, together with the outward tokens of loyalty to our King and Queen, and the witness given by the splendid array to the continuity of our English tradition. Church and State were superbly united.

CHAPTER XXI

Sandringham

r HAPPENED THAT I preached once or twice in Sandringham Church efore 1910 when I went as Bishop to Norwich. In those early days : was a village church, with suitable accommodation for the royal amily in the chancel to which a separate entrance gave access. In he tower at the west end sat the village children; it was, as it is ow, a small parish united with another neighbouring parish with its hurch not far away. Now a monument is in the tower, a larger eating is provided for the King's Household, and the chancel with its ouching and interesting memorials is richly embellished. There is ecorated and gilded panelling all round the east end: there is a silver ulpit given by an American admirer of King Edward VII, after his eath, who also presented a silver altar, on the face of which in the ame dull silver are the royal arms with an angel on either side, and bove a silver reredos representing our Lord with His disciples. There ; nothing flamboyant in these embellishments: they harmonize with he structure of the church, though of course they have changed its imple character as I first knew it. I remember one Sunday morning King George V spending quite a long time in showing me, in the hall f the House, the new and valuable church plate. (The church is pproached by an avenue of firs from the House.)

Sandringham was King Edward's country home—where he was ot only the King but the Squire; the Squire first, then the King.

The grounds were attractively laid out, with beauty and precision. o this day the public are generously admitted to them, and the small ntrance fees go to charitable purposes. King Edward had a great ye for detail, and those who had any responsibility for his expenditure lmost dreaded any day which he was able to spend on the estate, vhen he would propose costly improvements and fresh plans.

The House is not very attractive to look at—red brick with stone acings, it has the true air of an imposing Victorian villa that has been nlarged and adapted once or twice not very successfully; passages upstairs are too narrow; the main entrance, from which Queen Alexandra used to feed the birds, opens into a central hall surrounded y a gallery leading to rooms on the upper level. This hall—with ables added one to another as need required—used to be the scene of ea, at which in her time Queen Mary presided: the dining-room and lrawing-room and other rooms lead into it. In a corner of it was a veighing chair, in which any of the guests in the House could be weighed. I remember years ago finding it indicated that in year and a half my weight had gone up a stone and a half, and mentioned this to the King, who I thought would be an authority o. the matter, for King George V once remarked that in his Father' family there was a tendency to stoutness, though his own weight wa always about ten stone. King Edward exclaimed that the increas was excessive: "Too much! Too much!" He disguised his ow 'stoutness' by an ingenious plan of fastening his frock coat with link, which made the coat go further, so to speak, than if it had bee buttoned.

There was always an easy but dignified little ceremony whe the King and Queen came last into the room in which their guest and household were assembled to receive them and to bow and curtse their respects before they entered the dining-room, which commande a charming view of the park, towards the church. The dinner wa not a heavy banquet. After it the bagpipes were played around th table.

It is not easy to describe the effect of the arrival of King Edward perhaps from London, in time for dinner. One felt that the whol place was alive and eager with hurried coming and going of attendants a spirit of keenness was in the air. He imparted a sense of welcom and respectful ease. I remember once when he pressed me to tak some liqueur, and I had refused it, saying I was a pledged abstaine he met me with the good-humoured rejoinder "Ah, but this is stomachic." He was not always an easy person with whom to carr on a conversation, for he was given to express himself by question which required a direct and limited reply.

For the Sunday before his death he had run down to Sandringhan with Sir D. Probyn, and his intimate friend Lord Redesdale, th famous sylviculturist, to consider some planting. He attende church, as usual, in the morning; and it was noticed that on that da he did not lean forward as usual but knelt down in his place at th end of the narrow pew. . . .

Queen Alexandra added a charm wherever she moved; there wa a grace and friendliness in her bearing which won all hearts.

I like to recall that one day when I was at Sandringham, it wa Queen Alexandra's Rose Day: there was in the hall a tub with bush of hand-made roses planted in it, and Queen Alexandra con siderately had a sprig plucked off it which she gave to me to wear I have it still.

Sandringham is in a beautiful part of Norfolk, and all the road round the park look trim and delightful with the uneven sandy slopes the rhododendrons, the plantations, the bracken, and the wide gras

argins to the roads: for Norfolk is not a flat country like much of
ambridgeshire. It has no high hills but it is undulating with pleasing
ariety. The district could never have looked more beautiful than
n the day in January, 1936, when King George V started on his last
urney from his country home to London. We had a touching
neral service in the church. The pews were crowded with neigh-
ours, tenants and local friends; it was a gathering of affection and
ot a ceremonial function. We sang the hymn "Peace, perfect peace"
–"A favourite of his," as poor dear Queen Mary whispered to me
hile we waited in the Lych-gate. Then everyone started, most
alking, some motoring, in the procession of some miles to Wolferton
ation. There had been a hoar frost during the night, picking out
ith white the fir trees and the grass at the sides of the road. The
inter sun shone brightly with sparkling light. On the rising ground
ear the railway station large crowds from Norfolk were gathered,
ut there was still the touch of home-farewell which would have been
npossible in the London streets or in the stream of people who
assed through Westminster Hall on those melancholy days after
he King's death.

CHAPTER XXII

Queen Mary

UEEN MARY IS exceedingly beloved, and through the personal
ffection she evokes, her public influence has long been very great.
t is likely that the regard in which she is held steadied the general
ttitude in the anxious time of the abdication of Edward VIII. She
s one of those who have grown and developed as the years have
one by. Juvenal has referred to those people who have received
heir education in the school of life (*vita didicere magistra*). She
s one of them. From the beginning there was something specially
ttractive in her. When she was a girl her mother said of her to
 neighbour—"She is a pearl". A sister in a family of brothers often
vins a sweetness and unselfishness of her own; her mother had much
o say, and that, too, tends to create for a listening daughter a place
f her own in the family circle. Her brothers were at Wellington,
ut not in my time. People have sometimes spoken of her as shy,
ut 'quiet' would be a truer word, describing a quality derived from

those early years. Shy persons are often nervous and awkward
That could never be said of Queen Mary. If she relapses into silence
it is a contented silence, which does not harass others with any
misgivings. It was no doubt difficult for her to step from her home
life into the public gaze when she suddenly received general attention
and presentations were made to her, in view of her coming marriage
I have heard one of her first speeches and her confusion painfully
described. Was not such diffidence only natural and becoming? But
she gradually grew into her new position, which she has adorned with
her capacity, her good sense, and her power to come near to all whom she
knows well or merely sees on passing occasions. Her quick eye takes in
everything and everybody. Her appearance and bearing, always
pleasing, came in later years to be stately. On a great day her presence
would be magnificent. I confess that my own feeling towards her is a
blend of respect and admiration, with real affection and a grateful sense
of easy companionableness.

I have had many opportunities of observing her, and she has
shown singular kindness to my wife and me and our little girl, whose
godmother she became by her own proposal. It was very like her
to say that though the child should bear the name of Mary she might
be called by one of her other names. , Till we despatched our small
daughter to America when the war came, Queen Mary always sent
her a lovely Christmas present exactly suited to her years on each
occasion: this is the more remarkable as every year she used to send
hundreds of Christmas presents in all directions. She was really
disturbed if anyone felt overlooked. We still receive her Christmas
cards.

When she spent Christmas at Sandringham with King George V
they showed together a true neighbourliness to the clergy and others
in their immediate vicinity. I remember the King laughing with her
over the excessive prices she had paid for odds and ends at a sale
which a retiring bachelor parson held of some of his goods. She is
quick to see the funny side of the little incidents of ordinary life
I might very well have told that at one of my visits to Sandringham I
found that my man had not packed up any clean collars for me. I
did the best I could for two days with the one I was wearing. When
I went upstairs to the private sitting-room of the King and Queen to
say good-bye the conversation turned to a guest who had just left
Naturally I felt at a disadvantage when among other things the King
remarked that he had looked so clean.

When first I used to go to Sandringham, they lived at York
Cottage, a small house at a little distance from the big house. This
was still occupied by Queen Alexandra, to whom Queen Mary showed

wonderful self-effacing considerateness, in order that Queen
exandra should not feel too acutely that her days as Queen were
er.

Queen Mary often came to the Palace at Norwich. An amusing
cident occurred on her first visit, when she brought with her some
the young princes, then small boys, and we went to the Castle
useum. There she called their attention to some tigers (not very
od specimens) which "Papa had shot in India". The visit was
cognito and I had said nothing about it. We all know that Queen
ary always sticks to her umbrella as regularly as she wears her
que. When we were going into the Castle the hall porter asked her
give up the umbrella. She declined, but he respectfully pressed
e regulation. Then the Queen told me to disclose to him who
e was. What a shock for the porter! Another time she came to
some shopping. We took her to one or two shops, in which her
onderful memory and her acquaintance with furniture revealed
elf. She picked out pieces that would suit well for the comfort
d adornment of some unimportant rooms in certain royal residences.
olyrood exhibits her taste and the way she has seen how to transfer
ccessfully articles from one house to another. Her taste is backed
· her historical knowledge and the attention with which she remem-
rs what she has seen and learnt. It is all done with a light touch:
thing pedantic, no affectation.

One day at lunch she immediately recognized portions of a silver
t dessert service the loan of which my wife secured in her honour.
was the Leopold pattern. Three sets were, I believe, made, one
: the King of the Belgians, and my wife's great grandmother secured
second, which remained in the family. (This King, Queen Victoria's
cle, is not to be confused with Leopold II of Congo ill-fame; the
chbishop in Belgium felt it his duty to see the latter and denounce
e grave blots upon his private life. But the King got the best of
e interview when, after listening courteously, he said, "My dear
chbishop, I have heard exactly the same of you, but I did not
lieve a word of it.")

Queen Mary sees all round a subject and is never so engrossed with
e aspect of it as to forget the wider implications. Her knowledge
affairs makes her very wise. She is not, however, so cautious as
be unwilling, in conversation, to commit herself to an opinion, and
ll comment in praise or blame, trusting those to whom she is talking
th a free expression of her likes and dislikes. She appreciates,
d by her example uplifts family life.

One day, opening a new part of the Norfolk and Norwich Hospital,
e learnt that the name of the designer of the key had not been put

on the list of presentations. Unwilling to disappoint him,
insisted that he should be found, and then graciously complimen
him.

I could not but see how deeply she was affected at the Coronat
of King George VI and Queen Elizabeth—for my seat was facing he
And no wonder! For memories and disappointments, hopes a
regrets must have crowded into her mind. But she has risen super
above the limitations of her life; she has nobly used the opportuni
that have come her way. Her personality has secured in no mer
courtly manner the homage of us all. England and the Empire o
which she has travelled is deeply indebted to her for her inspirat
and for her example in public and home life, and they know it.

CHAPTER XXIII

Some Friends and Associates

I HAVE MADE many friends as the years have gone by, some old
some younger than myself. These friendships have been a last
possession, especially from my days at Marlborough onwards. I v
on intimate terms with the boys at Wellington. They often come
in the street to speak to me now, and some of them would come a
stay with me in Norwich. But there the first place must be given
the clergy *and their wives*. It is not right that a bishop should lo
upon the clergy as if he were merely the head of an ecclesiasti
department; he belongs to the laymen and the children too. I ha
constantly received the greatest kindness from laymen in this p
of the world. They have offered liberal hospitality, and in my ea
years especially, when the ground to be covered was larger, but r
exclusively then, I often have stayed a few days, accompanied
my secretary and chauffeur, in their houses, so that I might radi
out to engagements in various parishes. I have in this way come i
close contact with some of the homes in Norfolk and Suffolk. Anc
is not only the leading laymen with whom I have come into associati
I have liked to know that anyone could turn to me as a friend a
guide. But naturally I saw more of the clergy, and they alwa
wrote to me friendly letters. It was a joy to see the manner in wh
the best of them commended themselves to their people, not w
just an official touch, but through their godly lives of Christian servi

GROUP AT THE PALACE ON THE OCCASION OF THE NORWICH MUSICAL FESTIVAL, 1924

Reading from left: The Earl of Leicester, the Earl of Albemarle, Cora the Countess of Strafford, Lady Cynthia Colville, Lady Joan Verney, Mrs. Herbert Smith.

The Marchioness of Cholmondeley, the Countess of Albemarle, the Bishop of Norwich, the Queen, the Duchess of York, the Countess of Leicester, Lady Hastings.

RUIN OF GATEWAY TO PALACE
BANQUETING HALL

NORWICH CATHEDRAL FROM THE
PALACE GARDENS, AND THE
PALACE CHAPEL

For their wives my wife had a Clergy Wives' Fellowship,
couraging them to see something of one another, and that not
ly through parochial work. She had also a society for the daughters,
cing them now and then on excursions, and providing a type-
itten magazine to which they contributed some really excellent
icles and drawings; each number was circulated to all the members.
ice a year all the wives who belonged to the Fellowship would come
the Palace and join in a happy afternoon or day. Besides tran-
ting the business, they would listen to a talk or hear some music,
., and after tea there would be a crowded service in the chapel with
cial prayers and an address. These gatherings gave me an oppor-
ity for making friends, and I could tell them how deeply we were
ebted to them for their devotion in their ceaseless round of occupa-
n, keeping them busy on Sundays and weekdays alike among the
mbers of the flock, sick or well, young and old; and taking with
m the touch of sympathy and family feeling.

One would hear in unexpected ways of the goodness of the clergy.
s truly absurd to speak of them as if they only did one day's work
seven. Some of them are, I know, touchy and self-important and
professional, and some live life without much discipline and regu-
ty in it. In the country you may sometimes find them wearing
pers and going about unshaven. But this does not represent the
ole man, nor the whole body of the clergy. Throughout its length
l breadth our land is indebted to them, and the blessing of God is
their gallant work carried on day by day, often among discourage-
nts. I have been very happy among them and have greatly valued
ir friendship.

I remember very well, in the days before the Church Assembly was
up, moving in the House of Lords a Bill for reorganizing the scheme
eady in existence for uniting benefices. I explained that in country
tricts everything rested upon the shoulders of the clergy in a way
recognized by the general public; anyone who needed guidance
things great or small would turn to the parson. In the war of
4–1918 he would often be the only one at hand to break the news
bereavements. He would have to make clear the forms which
ald have to be signed; to offer suggestions for the right type of work
the growing lads and girls of the parish. It is he who, with his
e, would hold the parish together as one community, making
nds with them all.

Such work takes time and is exacting; the people are not clear in
ard to their requirements and they are naturally put off by a man
appears to be in a hurry and will not quietly listen to the story
ch they tell in their own unhurried and obscure manner. Some of

D

these country parsons hold services for hikers and cyclists and othe
coming from a distance. Sometimes they will invite such people, wl
are out for some exercise on Sunday, to drop in to the morning servi
of the parish without making special arrangements for them,
providing forms of service at which no one else is present.

The clergy often take special pains over Sunday Schools, whe
they possess a freedom for giving spiritual lessons which they do n
find; for example, when I was anxious to enable children of the Chur
of England and of the Free Churches to pray together in August, 19
when the war was looking very serious, I collected them all into r
own garden on a Sunday with the Lord Mayor of Norwich and a Fr
Church Minister present, and each gave an address. The band of t
Salvation Army accompanied this simple service. It was said th
there were eight thousand children present.

Where parishes are united the clergy have to take great pains
see that there is a good Sunday School in each of them. Here, on
more, their wives or other lady superintendents are able to keep thir
devoutly going if the clergyman has to be away in the other of
parishes. Certainly in the country the clergyman is never off du
and it is far easier for the man in a town to make arrangements witl
neighbour for attending to any duty that may suddenly arise. He h
above all, the opportunity to make friends. Passing from the cler
and their wives, I have to be thankful for many other friends.
suppose I have inherited from my father and my mother some facil
for getting alongside those who have served me, or have been good
me in their own crafts and callings.

I have had intimate friends on our line (the L.N.E.R.), and mu
value their affection, and am personally indebted to them for th
goodness and eagerness to oblige. There is a very high standard
service among them; a tradition handed down from the days of Lo
Claud Hamilton, when he was chairman of the line. It is just the sa
in the Great Eastern Hotel, where it has always felt very much l
coming home, so real and warm has been the welcome.

I carried into my episcopal days a very great interest in hospi
work, and have received much personal consideration and ski
attention from those members of the remarkable staff of the Norf
and Norwich Hospital, whose friendship I have been proud to enj

The Police Force has always been most considerate to me, an
have personal friends in the Chief Constable of the County (who v
'under' me at Wellington), and the Chief Constable of Norwich, v
has a Boys' Club, of which the fame has travelled far and wide.

I have always received great kindness from the gentlemen connec
with the Press. Sometimes people complain of the matter appear

the Press, while they forget its duty to the public, not least in the
uations created by the War. They are not aware how much dis-
imination is shown in the way of omitting the things which the
essmen might include, if they published all that they knew. They
ed, and they show, a careful self-control, except when, in some cases,
ter a death, or at the time of family misfortune, they intrude upon
e afflicted. One wonders what the English pressmen would have
ne if they had been appealed to when, in the disturbed days in
eland, my cousin, coming home late one night, saw his father with a
volver in his hand at the top of the stairs, and heard him say:
Vho is that? If you speak, I'll shoot."

The Press are very glad of any help one can give them. I remember,
ring the great agricultural strike in Norfolk some twenty years ago,
eir industry, good temper, and their eagerness that an amicable
ttlement should be reached. They came in their numbers to the
lace, where I had arranged a meeting for farmers and men, who
re for the most part in the agricultural fraternity, and on good terms
th one another. Often they have been at the same school, and still
rk side by side, undivided by trade secrets. Unfortunately, on this
casion unwise counsels prevailed, involving a loss all round. The
mense weight in forming public opinion which belongs to the
ovincial Press is underrated. In these days of paper shortage it
ıst need much editorial skill to co-ordinate the demands of local and
ternational interests. There are times when one is glad that some
ident has missed the vigilant eyes of the newspaper men. I had
iciated at the wedding of a girl who was a great friend of mine. It
ıs a pouring wet day and I had to hurry off to the House of Lords.
er mother said to me: "You must go in a car on such a day. There
e a lot of them waiting at the door; so do get into the first one you
e." I did so, and when I arrived at Westminster I found that
ıdvertently I had stepped into the bride's own car and had travelled
the way with a wedding shoe tied on to the back of it, but no one
d noticed this little mistake.

It is a happy consideration that so many papers, metropolitan and
al, publish weekly religious articles on a Saturday. Our own
stern Daily Press is very glad to do this, and every day prints a text
m the Bible.

CHAPTER XXIV

Letters

WHEN I RETIRED from the bishopric of Norwich our excellent loc
paper, *The Eastern Daily Press*, to which I referred just now, w
good enough, even in these days of paper shortage, to give rather
full account of my Episcopate. It is not for me to give any opini
upon what was written, except to say that I, myself, should ha
spoken fully of the help I received from my Assistant Bishop, t
Dean, the Archdeacons, and the Rural Deans. The account contain
some friendly references to my habits in letter-writing, of which th
said: "The Bishop will long be remembered for the singular charm
his letters. To few is bestowed in such measure the gift of writir
Whatever their nature, whether of business or concerned with t
deep things of life, his letters carried and carry an indefinable quali
which places them outside the category of ordinary correspondence
I do not suggest that this is an accurate description of the way I de
with correspondence, but I should like to be able to write letters aft
the fashion described. It is a different method from that employ
by a bishop of a previous generation whose daughters acted as secr
taries; it was said that when a clergyman in the diocese wrote to a
for the bishop's consent to some plan or to a form of service, all
received back was a post card, written by one of the daughters, sayin
"Pa says you mustn't."

In handling letters it is always wise to let your correspondent kno
that you have read and grasped the business items, and before a rep
is posted you will read over his letter again with what you ha
just written to be sure that it will be plain to him that you have n
missed any of his points, or any of the arguments he has put forwar
Those who use a typewriter and dictate their letters will be care!
to remember that there is a temptation to write and elaborate
excess in too diffuse a manner.

Some of the letters of Archbishop Lord Davidson (who may
called a veritable specialist in dictating letters and memorand
certainly tended to diffuseness. His mind seemed to work along t
full and formal sentences to which a typescript is prone. But ev
when you dictate, you can add a few words in your own hand a
perhaps a friendly postscript. This will bring you alongside t
person to whom you are writing and give a human touch to your wor
however businesslike the earlier part of your letter has been. It is

istake to be lengthy. Other people who receive your letters may be
ısy and may well prefer a succinct letter, if you are careful to see
at it is not curt but still retains an air of human sympathy.

It is a common mistake to confuse importance with urgency.
`equently a matter of real importance may require care, attention,
ıd deliberation, and will allow of these being given. This confusion
»plies not only to the writing of letters but to interviews, etc. It is
` no means certain that in every case a matter of importance must
dealt with immediately; it may even be that the question will
rt itself out and offer an opportunity for a fuller and wiser discussion,
there is no hurry in deciding it. A matter of far less importance
ıy be much more urgent, some small thing may need to be done at
ce, if the chance of doing it at all is not to be lost.

When you are going to write a letter on a matter which involves
nuine sentiment and feeling for yourself, it is prudent to reflect in
ıat place and in what frame of mind it is likely to be received. If
u are writing to a man whose occupation involves the receipt of a
eat many letters, and is eager to keep his head above water by
aling with them as rapidly as possible, it would be a mistake to send
him a letter full of feeling, at any rate, to his business premises.
ch a letter should be sent to his home address, where he will have
obably a better opportunity of listening to the fullness of your own
art with a sympathetic understanding on his side.

It is a mistake to write complaints in a letter, especially if they
er to your correspondent. I have known a man who used to say:
always like to consider how my letter would read if it came up in
ase in Court." This, perhaps, was going too far, for it would make
ters dull if everybody everywhere followed such a rule. But it is
ıe *litera scripta manet* ('the written word remains'), and this makes it
ıre seemly that criticisms of a personal character should be spoken,
d have no permanence given to them by appearing in a letter.

In a general way no one now asks for detailed news, nor are they
erested in the descriptions that one can write about places and
nery that can be better portrayed in a guide-book, nor are they
erested in comments on current affairs such as the newspaper
ovides; though, of course, it is quite different if personal and inter-
ing remarks can be made upon events of the day which could not
published in a paper for the world at large to read. It was different
old days when many of the events that were passing, say in London,
ly reached one who was living in the provinces through the full
ters of a friend residing in the Metropolis. Such old letters are
quently interesting to us to read now, and there may be occasions
m time to time for writing similar letters to-day; anyone who

proposes in a letter to describe a scene must make sure that wh
he has written is clear. It is easy when one is full of a subject
forget that, if one is writing about it to someone else, the writi
should be in such a manner that the whole tale can be understo
without any need of further information only known to the writ
Anyone receiving such a letter cannot borrow the keys which the writ
has in his own mind but happens not to have mentioned.

It is a mistake in a letter to say that there is no news and nothi
to write about: for that depends upon the things which will intere
the man or woman to whom you are writing. Not long ago a bish
who had considerable Colonial experience of a bishop's work, told r
that when he met soldiers from abroad who had come to Englan
especially if they came from one or other of those parts of the Empi
with which he was familiar, he quickly got into conversation with the
and in his own friendly manner enquired whether they were regular
writing home. If they said they were not, then he begged them to
so, because he knew for himself, and assured them of, the great intere
which would attach to even a few lines written by them to those
their distant homes. He was, of course, aware how easy it is to g
out of the habit of writing regularly and then to omit letters altogeth
The truth is that letters written by those for whom we care do n
depend for their interest upon the news which can be more or l
gathered from the public prints: the real charm lies in the wri
coming in heart near to those who are thinking of him. An allusi
to happy memories which they share will bring them far nearer togeth
than a bald recital of any facts which might be classed as news.
very few words, spoken from heart to heart, go a long way with tho
who are bound to us by family ties or by an old friendship which pr
vides us with intimate recollections, that belong to ourselves, and
less to those from whom time and distance have parted us. Aga
absent friends will value much more highly than mere news yc
own opinion on something you have read; for it will reveal to the
how your mind is working, and they may find a pleasure in getti
hold of the same book, and discovering whether they think as you
about it, or the passages you may have mentioned.

Arthur Benson was a prince among letter-writers. Sometimes
wrote too many, and I am not now speaking of his desire to get
the bottom of some misunderstanding between him and his frien
but rather of the kind of letter which he would write to me, full
friendly observation and insight, going beneath the surface a
making one feel that one was really by his side, and near his hea
and that his sympathy was very genuine and close. I had hac
slight acquaintance with him through several years, and though

er met, his not infrequent letters on various occasions warmed my
ings towards him, and I felt that I had won a friend. I should
: to be able to write letters which could establish a friendship
h some person unknown by face to me. Later on Benson and I
get to know one another personally, and this ripened a friendship,
:ady made by letter, into something more intimate and affectionate.
letters to me betokened the same considerateness which induced
1 in a general company to make much of anyone who seemed to
dull and out of it, and led him, as I remember, on one occasion,
help out a young man who, though knowing nothing of the subject,
astantly interposed with a foolish remark when two older and abler
n were discussing a matter of importance. Benson, with his adroit
nd, managed to make every one of these feeble interruptions appear
be relevant, only so slightly changing them that the young speaker
l not observe that Benson was cleverly befriending him.

I may add that I have found printed letters a useful medium for
nmunicating with sets of people to whom I had something to say.
the last war I used to write, now and again, printed letters to muni-
n workers in Norwich and the diocese, each distributed in many
ndreds of copies. I would sometimes express my own opinions on a
bject and ask of them whether they agreed with me or no. Sometimes
wrote a letter to the land girls, for we had many of them among us,
ough of course not in such numbers as there are to-day; they always
ike me as a particularly excellent type of war worker.

At the time of the National Mission of Repentance and Hope I
ote a printed letter for the children of the diocese, and on another
casion I wrote to them a letter encouraging interest in Foreign
issions, starting with some account of Stonehenge and alluding to
e fact that in earlier years England was a heathen country.

CHAPTER XXV

Prayer

ERE IS GREAT variety in a bishop's work. Many questions are
ferred to him and he is expected to speak or write on many interests
tside the common routine of his ordinary work. In this and some
the following chapters I have set down my own views on some
iritual issues that are always with us: Prayer, The Bible, The
rtainty of Faith.

Left to themselves, all men pray. Man is conscious of an unse
world and of powers that surround his life. His ideas may be degrad
or they may lead him to a noble worship of the true God who is (
of sight. For prayer we have the example of Our Lord and His (
ciples. Christ Himself could spend a whole night in prayer. St. P.
tells us to pray without ceasing, that is, never to discontinue our pray
We cannot go wrong if we follow their guidance. There are alwa
difficulties when the temporal reaches over to the eternal. But
can all use prayer to God without hesitation if our aim is to prom
His glory, and we remember Our Lord's teaching on the subject
God's care for us as Our Heavenly Father, and His interest in (
sparrow-like concerns.

It is quite easy to argue against prayer and to say that we can
suppose that God will change His purpose at our request. But (
prayer may well be something that falls within God's purposes.
may be that when we speak of God changing His purpose, we a
transferring into the timeless and infinite world difficulties that ar
from supposing that the eternal world (where God is) is comparable
the world of time, with its succession of events in which we are plac
To God there is neither a past nor future, only an eternal present

No doubt the answers to our prayers must be received by us
our own world, and, as we ourselves are placed, we may speak of
alteration from what we might have expected to occur if we had n
prayed. But it is a foolish thing to raise difficulties, if I may say
on God's side, which can only spring from our observation of t
answers to our prayers, as we see and receive those answers. C
business is to pray, not to argue with one another or with God, as
the manner in which He, on His side, can give us His answer.
probably means nothing if we begin to speak of what God 'would ha
done' if our prayer had not been uttered. In His eternal world there
no place for what 'would have happened', and our prayer, I repea
must not impute to God the limitations of our own life in which t
past and present and future, the hypothetical and the certain, a
distinct from one another. It is said that the arguments of those w
do not believe evaporate when they find themselves, or those who
they love, in grave or unexpected danger. Then they become li
other people and follow the normal instinct; even they sudden
learn to say: "Thou that hearest the prayer, unto Thee shall all fle
come."

If we are to have this child-like attitude to prayer we must belie
that it comprises definite petitions. To those petitions God, who
all wise and who is all loving, may say "No"; and it is possible for Hi
to answer these petitions in a manner that, at any rate at the momer

es not appear to correspond with what we have been asking. St.
ul's prayer for the removal of his thorn in the flesh was not literally
swered, but something better was granted in the assurance of the
fficiency of God's grace, and of His strength made perfect in the
ry weakness of His servant. Those who wait upon God will often
cover that He has not turned a deaf ear to what they have said,
d has given something more worth having. We can reverently
nk of Our Lord's prayer in Gethsemane, and of the Victory of the
oss which followed His drinking of the cup of agony.

It is irreverent and misguided to try to test the power of God to
swer prayer. Such a so-called prayer was offered by praying for
e recovery of the patients on one side of a ward in a hospital, and
t for the recovery of those on the other side. The prayer was not
swered. How could it be? It was based not on faith, but on the
k of it.

It is often stated that the word prayer must comprehend other
ms of turning to God, that in it are included meditation, the con-
mplation of God, and other attitudes towards Him. Such contem-
ation of God is something different from putting our requests before
m, and it may be that communion with Him, and the sense of the
esence of God, is something higher and deeper than asking Him
some special item. But prayer means prayer, and I see no good
confusing terms and in suggesting that when the Bible guides us
prayer it really means something else, something besides; this
ght reduce the strength and the expectancy of our prayer.

Those will pray best who can bring the mind of Christ to bear
on their petitions. For example, it is impossible for us to expect
answer to any malicious request, because we dare not offer any
tition that is against the will of God. I remember when I was
child thinking that the collect "Let Thy merciful ears, O Lord, be
en to the prayers of thy humble servants; and that they may
tain their petitions make them to ask such things as shall please
ee" was rather pointless. We know, however, that the Christian
rns to God in prayer in the Name of Christ, and we cannot suppose
at we can rightly attach that Name to any unworthy request.
at Name will, so to speak, sort out our prayers as well as give to
a full right of approach to the Throne of Grace. The mind of
rist must be supreme and the nearer we reach towards it the better
r prayers will be. This is what I had not seen when I was a small
y, and said to myself, "If, in any case, God is going to do what
eases Him, I do not see that there is any need for my prayers."
had not grasped that that collect does not rule out our praying at
, but leads us in the way of praying better prayers, prayers that

D*

are more likely to be answered in a manner that our heart desires should desire.

In the Lord's Prayer we ask for our daily bread, and it leads t[...] way for us not to exclude these temporal desires in drawing ne[...] to God. We make a mistake, therefore, if we leave out our earth[...] needs. But here we have to note that we cannot necessarily persua[...] others of our own assurance that God has heard us and helped [...] We may be quite certain in our own hearts that God has helped [...] according to our requests; but this kind of certainty need not, a[...] often does not, approve itself to others. We are wrong if we ma[...] an effort to convince them, especially when it is often the way [...] God to use common events and powers, based on science, like t[...] physician's skill, for the carrying out of His purposes, and many w[...] miss His hand where we see it and will attribute what has happen[...] to the ordinary course of events. On our part we can trace His acti[...] when we find that He has been employing the familiar laws of Natu[...] and the usual course of events so as to make them coincide with o[...] needs. There is nothing specially remarkable in finding a coin [...] the mouth of a fish; but it becomes remarkable if we catch such [...] fish at the very moment when we need that coin. It is not remarkab[...] if the prelude to a coming thunderstorm is found in the lightni[...] flash. Elijah's sacrifice on Mount Carmel may have been consum[...] by the lightning that came before the thunderstorm, which he watch[...] arising a little later when he had said to Ahab: "There is a sound [...] abundance of rain."

We must be careful that our prayers are not self-centred. T[...] most important part of prayer is intercession, and we know that t[...] last picture that we have of our Great High Priest in Heaven is th[...] He ever lives to make intercession for us. We must follow F[...] example. Our Lord's Great Prayer in the seventeenth chapter [...] John includes petitions for his disciples both at that time and dov[...] the ages. Let us stand by His side.

The question of prayers for the departed is rather a special on[...] Personally I believe that St. Paul, in the second epistle to Timoth[...] asks God's mercy for Onesiphorus after his death, but I do not desi[...] to cover the historical and doctrinal ground which any full treatme[...] of prayers for the dead would require. I am thinking of our existi[...] Prayer Book and some considerations following from its reserv[...] The prayer that we know now as the Prayer for the Church Milita[...] limits itself by its bidding. An earlier Prayer Book had the larg[...] heading: "The whole state of Christ's church," but in 1552 came t[...] restrictive words, "militant here in earth." In the last authoritati[...] revision, however, was added the final touching petition relating [...]

e faithful that, *with them* we may be made partakers of God's heavenly
ingdom. Here is a beautiful reference to the saints who have
ossed over, whom this prayer originally mentioned with greater
articularity and independently of the living.

Similarly in the Burial Service we pray that "we *with all* those that
e departed in the true faith of thy holy Name may have our perfect
onsummation and bliss." The dead are associated with the living.
a the Prayer of Oblation we pray "that by the merits and death of
y Son Jesus Christ we, and all thy whole church, may obtain
mission of sins and all other benefits of his passion." Some will
gard these words as limited by the present bidding before the prayer
r the whole state of Christ's Church militant here in earth. Others
ill regard the petition as once more stressing the fellowship between
e living and the dead.

There can be little doubt that the Church of England when it
lopted its present attitude to prayers for the dead had before it
asses for the dead, and indulgences, and was opposed to any sort of
1al transactions, however understood or misunderstood, in dealing
ith spiritual things here and hereafter.

On the one hand, therefore, the Church of England does not forbid
ayers for the dead (the matter has been so determined in the
cclesiastical Courts) but the Prayer Book contains no public prayers
viding the dead from the living. Many will rejoice that our Prayer
ook scheme of intercession emphasizes in this way the Communion
Saints.

> *One family we dwell in Him,*
> *One church above, beneath;*
> *Though now divided by the stream,*
> *The narrow stream of death.*

We can rightly pray for what we rightly desire, but in public
ayer we are wisely on our guard against dangerous developments
hich seem to be creeping back to-day, lest they should lead to old
uses. Holy Scripture is very silent about new opportunities in
e beyond.

Sometimes we do find in contemporary services this isolation of
e deceased. Many would shrink from any form of petition which
ems to thrust their dearest into some lonely place in the under-
orld, as it were for special treatment, from which those who are
ft behind are excluded. In Christ we are still one family, and very
ose to one another. What a real and happy consolation for the
oken heart of the mourner! An anxious friend, who has been
llowing step by step all that can be heard about one who is very

dear, now hears that he is missing. Perhaps letters posted earlier sti
arrive and deepen the love between them, for in them they read
happenings and memories which both have shared. Then com
news of his death. The mourners cannot bear to remove him eve
for a moment from their unbroken fellowship in Christ, the Lord
both the dead and the living. In their new acute sorrow they fir
comfort in knowing that the old affectionate comradeship is mai
tained in a heavenly form. Why should the memorial service pla
him into the far away?

I may just repeat that if our present burial service is ever fe
to be unsatisfactory a greater liberty is allowed in regard to it than
other occasional offices. When the persons responsible for the buri
request it, a clergyman may use special forms approved by t
Ordinary.

CHAPTER XXVI

Bible Reading

IT HAS BEEN said, and quite rightly, that nothing could do more f
our English life and character than that the Bible should once mo
come back into its own. People do not now read and know t
Bible as they did long ago. There are various reasons for this, o
of them of course being that there is now a vast number of book
journals and magazines—some good, some bad—which people ca
read according to their tastes, whereas the Bible held a unique positic
in the years after it was translated into the English language and ma
available to all. Before that time it only reached the common peop
according to the will and the teaching of the priests. When peop
do turn to it and read it they find that it has not lost its spell.

For those who will take the time and give the trouble to read
every day, or at least every week, there is no disappointment in stor
I have constantly, in the days of this war and of the last war, giv
a copy of St. Luke's gospel, which has been called the most beautif
book in the world, or of some other portion of Holy Scripture to t
soldiers whom I have confirmed and have urged them not to mi
the chance of reading it. Lately I put into the front page of ea
copy a few words mentioning that I had had the honour to carry t

ible in the Coronation Procession in Westminster Abbey: In the rvice that followed, the Bible was presented to the King with the ords:

We present you with this Book, the most valuable thing that this world ffords. Here is wisdom: this is the royal Law; these are the lively racles of God.

One day during the last war I was talking in the garden at the alace to an old pupil of mine who was just going to the Front, and gave to him a small book of the New Testament which he could sily carry and suggested to him to read a little bit of it, a few verses, very day. Later on he came to stay with me again after he had een wounded at the Front, and he told me that he had followed my dvice, and wherever he had been he had kept the small booklet ith him, and had not failed to read it daily. That is the story of young officer, and he must be one of many.

I remember the way in which the then Commander-in-Chief, the ld Duke of Cambridge, read his daily portion of Scripture. When he as staying in a country house to make one of a shooting party, as sual he read the Bible after breakfast, before going out. If he was nterrupted during his reading by anyone who came to tell him that ne guns were ready to start out, the intruder would be met by a volley f the vehement language of which he was a master. (But in contrast such impatience, a passing reference must be made to the friendliness nd geniality he showed when he came to Wellington for the athletic orts.) His father, we may note, listened attentively in church to the ading of the Scriptures, and here as elsewhere in the service he ould make aloud his own comments. When he heard the story of acchæus who said: "The half of my goods I give to the poor," the uke exclaimed: "Very liberal, very liberal"; but when Zacchæus dded: "If I have taken anything from any man by false accusation restore him fourfold," the Duke protested, "too much, too much." n another occasion, when the clergyman said, "Let us pray for in," the Duke remarked aloud: "The wind must change first." n saying this, unconsciously he illustrated the way in which, as I ave said, God answers prayer, for He commonly uses the ordinary ays of Nature, or men, in doing this, but he uses them in connection ith the human needs put before Him, and at the time when His uppliants are turning to Him for His help.

The Bible is a great book for great times, and it is no cause for onder if more are reading it now, though many well-bound Bibles ppear in salvage collections. We find that in a unique manner the

many books of the Bible, which originated at various stages in th
development of Christianity, in the end came to have a close coheren
together so that these various books have made one volume. Th
very word 'Bible' makes this plain. Strictly speaking, the Lati
means 'books' (in the plural), but it came to be used as a singula
word. The Unity of the Bible comes from its one theme: From th
beginning to the end it speaks of God, and gives to Him the fir
place in men's hearts and conduct. The prophets were constant
calling their hearers and readers to God. The historical books we
not written fully to present the outward history of the people; in th
Hebrew Bible they are more sympathetically called "the form
prophets": these histories were written still with the idea of puttin
God first. And the history recorded in this way is the history of
nation and of the development of its life, with a divine commentar
written concurrently upon it.

People now speak of the life of nations and wish they could fir
some authoritative guidance for directing a nation's life: for a natio
has a corporate life gathering up or consummating the personal liv
of the individuals who compose it. We have already this guidan
in the Old Testament. If we take, for example, the book of Amo
into our hands we can learn what is the right standard for a peopl
showing them what to do and what to avoid. Equally we see in th
Bible the touch of God on personal character and how He could exa
and beautify it. His judgments too upon personal failures are clea
The Bible speaks of men and women. It is not a book of Philosoph
or Ritual: Ritual has its place but it is no mere routine. The ritu
of the Day of Atonement given in the Book of Leviticus offers a mo
touching account of God's dealings with a sinful people. We kno
Holman Hunt's picture of *The Scapegoat*. Human nature is the sam
in all ages. Terms of philosophy change their meaning. Ritual, to
is not stable. But the Bible, speaking to us through the life o
individuals and of a whole nation, is always contemporary with ever
generation. In both the Old Testament and the New Testamen
the Bible presents us with a gallery of portraits which appeals
us all and not least to children, who from these portraits learn abou
God and about his influence on human life.

Our Lord was reared upon the Old Testament. The Book whic
helped Him can never be obsolete. He constantly refers to it an
employs its language. It supplied Him with the phrases in whic
to express his deepest yearnings in His Passion. We observe in th
record of His temptation how He used the Bible phrases to confro
and conquer the tempter. Those who use the Bible in this mann
learn the secret of its power; too many who turn to the Bible at a

the present time prefer to read about it than to read its pages with
their own eyes and to bring them, as Our Lord did, right into the
actualities of their own movements.

The Bible reveals the nature of man as well as of God. Man was
created in the image of God, and was meant to grow after His likeness
until the human race should be crowned and consummated by One
who would be perfect man and Himself Divine. But mankind fell
before the onset of sin and self-will, and the types of the Old Testament
and the facts of the New Testament and the interpretation put upon
them show to us the way in which, through Christ, God has redeemed
mankind: for we have to remember that sin is an intruder. It may
be universal, but it does not belong to the essence of man's nature, and
Christ, who was the one perfect Man, was able to take upon Himself
the sin of the world and to restore man to His high calling. He lived
and died for those whom He was not ashamed to call His brethren.
He was no alien victim brought in to stand between the wrath of
God and sinful men. He was one of ourselves, only perfect; and by
taking to Himself the whole of human nature He has given to each and
all a place in His completed work. He is the Representative man
and we all potentially have a foothold in Christ's achievement, and
St. Paul is fully justified in constantly using his favourite phrase
"in Christ".

Christ being truly human and truly Divine has by His incarnation
united man with God. Right away then from its beginning the
Old Testament points forward to Christ, who beyond all the teaching
of the prophets brought God before the eyes of men in a perfect human
life; when we ask what is God like we turn our eyes to Christ the
Lord: He that hath seen me hath seen the Father. In the Old
Testament we shall not find the standards of the New. But, bit by
bit, the Old Testament shows a growing apprehension of the Being
and the claims of God. God himself does not change, but man's
understanding of Him does develop. We cannot expect to find in
the early days of Israel's career anything to correspond with the
Beatitudes or the style and level of Christian character which Christ's
disciples have set before us; and this Christian character is derived
from Christ Himself dwelling through the Holy Spirit in our lives.
It is not only His example and teaching we have to direct us: He is
indeed the Way but He is also the Life. "Christ liveth in me," writes
St. Paul, "and the life which I now live in the flesh I live by the faith
of the Son of God, who loved me and gave himself for me. It is all
"in Christ". St. Paul did not seek a system of ethics to rule his
conduct; Christ within, the Living Christ, gave the guidance and the
power. One of the marks of Christ's disciples has been that they did

not begin by revolutionising the world, but they brought the min
of Christ to bear upon it as it was, and diffused a devotion to Him
and a direct dependence on Him, that undermined the basis of the
institutions which were incompatible with the mind of Christ. The
did not, for instance, attack the system of slavery, but taught such
whole-hearted brotherhood of men in Christ as made slavery im
possible among fellow Christians.

The Bible that will help us is the Bible in the form in which
believers have received it. It is a fascinating study to try to se
from what sources and in what manners the Bible reached its presen
form. But there is nothing particularly spiritual in this, though o
course it removes some difficulties and perplexities and the shock o
some contradictions, if we discover that on the literary side it is no
everywhere a homogeneous whole. But it is the spiritual voice o
the Bible which matters, and if we seek or hear that, the Bible ha
fulfilled its purpose for us one by one. There is no reason to condemn
the way in which other people reach that message provided that the
do not impose upon others their particular methods; nor must we
impose ours upon them. Any reading that is reverent and charitable
and looks for God in Christ will lead the learned or the simple to Him

We regard the inspiration of the Bible as an inspiration of author
and not of phrases. Nor is there any reason to say that other writer:
of other literatures have no inspiration: God has used for His pur
poses all the noble talents of men in all lands. But no one can deny
that the Bible speaks of God in a manner all its own, and in it we have
a unique inspiration. It is in our own hearts that we find a verifica
tion of the truth of its claims. Why then concentrate upon its diffi
culties? There are plenty of them, as there are plenty in all other
ancient literature, and it is no sign of wisdom or progress to write a
large question mark over its narratives and teaching. It spoils the
use of the Bible, for children, constantly to suggest to them that we
cannot everywhere be sure of its precision on the earthly side. This
would puzzle them with unprofitable discussions, though it may be
well for them to hear the extent to which modern excavations in
Palestine have supported the statements of the Bible. When I was
young it was questioned whether writing prevailed in the Holy Land
at the time of Moses. Now it is known that in that part of the East
it was in use before his day. Great discoveries have been made in and
near Jericho, confirming the Bible record of its capture. We want to
find in the Bible a friend and a guide. As young people develop they
may become sincerely puzzled over some literary or historical or
scientific points. There are plenty of books and commentaries to
which we can refer them, if they are seriously disquieted. But many

ision should be undertaken, a revision of the revised with only the
portant changes made in the Revised Version grafted on or into the
thorized. But who shall say what change is, and what is not,
portant? Are the alterations that have followed upon textual
ticism to be regarded as important or unimportant, or shall some
introduced and not others? I, for one, could not attempt to draw
line. Such a proposal to exclude some of the changes made in the
vised Version was once made in the presence of Bishop Westcott
d backed up by illustrations. "Why," said the critic, "why change
preposition in the phrase 'the gift of God is eternal life through
us Christ our Lord': why change 'through 'into 'in'?" To Bishop
stcott the change seemed important because eternal life is life *in*
rist: it is not a gift to us for His sake, but life in union with Him.
ho, then, can pronounce which are the changes that are significant,
ich the insignificant? If we keep the two books side by side there
no occasion to choose, and in many cases to spoil, the flow of the
guage of the Authorized Version by tampering with the words
th whose beauty we are familiar; we can, if we please, check the
e version by the other. There has been in the revision too great an
ort made to use the same English word in the places where the same
eek word is found, or to assimilate the rendering of a phrase occurring
re than once so as to make the passages containing it to correspond.
e Revisers have not been the slaves of their rule to use the same
glish word to render the same Greek word, but the rule was before
em. And perhaps it would be true to say that they have in many
ses sacrificed phrases to words, and feeling to logic. The Authorized
rsion (especially in contrast to the precisions of modern scholarship)
ned at and succeeded in producing a masterpiece of literature, as
ll as an adequate rendering. I have said elsewhere:

"However much new and better renderings may have removed
fficulties from the study of the Scriptures, the changes made by the
visers represent a very small fraction in the whole translation.
e Bible has determined the teaching of the National Church: it has
tered as a strong formative influence into the development of all
at is best in our English character." Anything then which concerns
e Bible is very dear to Englishmen, and I once suggested in con-
ocation that the work of the two companies of Revisers might, and
deed should, be commemorated by some suitable recognition in the
rusalem Chamber at Westminster where the meetings were held.
would be sad if the story of all the toil involved, and the names
those who took part, were forgotten. In this regard one would like
know that the Jerusalem Chamber would always be a shrine of
anksgiving, where in each generation men might enter into the

words with which the Old Testament Revisers concluded their labou
"with a feeling of deep thankfulness to Almighty God, and the earne
hope that their endeavours may, with His blessing, tend to a clea
knowledge of the Old Testament Scriptures", and into those of t
New Testament Revisers who to their thanksgiving added the pray
that: "The Gospel of our Lord and Saviour Jesus Christ may
more clearly and more freshly shown forth to all who shall be read
of this Book."

Speaking more specially of the New Testament, references to t
textual criticism of the Bible may be more easily grasped if I s
something about the literary search for a good manuscript, for
find that the meaning of the word 'good' in this respect is not clea
apprehended, and our recent acquisition of the *Codex Sinaiticus* bea
upon the significance of the word 'good' in this connection. The fir
excitement of our obtaining this great manuscript has now di
away. Everyone knows that it is *there* and safe, after all the vicis
tudes through which it has passed in the last hundred years. T
Government made a big grant for the purchase; but so great was t
interest taken in acquiring this famous manuscript for the natio
that a very large number of small contributors gladly sent what th
could to make up the sum required to secure it. England now ow
three of the five great Greek transcripts of Holy Scripture known
exist in the world: two are in London, one in Cambridge (written
Latin as well as in Greek).

It is, however, one thing to be pleased with our possessions, anoth
to understand and appreciate them. You will sometimes find t
owner of a great mansion who knows little about the treasures
contains from the æsthetic point of view. So with these manuscript
When we say that they are the best manuscripts, there are those wh
will start with our own English New Testament, and say: "But wh
change its words, or the Greek words which stand behind the English
To them the best manuscript is the one which, when translated, giv
the phrases they like best, or to which they are accustomed. I
reality the important thing is to discover what the author wrote. H
might have written something else: he might have written what u
would like better. But what *did* he write? The best manuscrip
are those which enable us most nearly to discover his words. It
not easy to do this, and we shall apprehend why it is difficult if w
observe what happened with these old manuscripts.

The author dictated a gospel or a letter. The pages he wrote ar
no longer in existence. But a few people copied them. These copie
were again copied by others. And this process went on through th
centuries. All was done by hand before printing was invented.

In copying a document mistakes are constantly made. A word will be omitted or written twice. The eye catches a phrase that happens to be used in one line and then again a few lines later; the words in between are accidentally left out. A scribe copying a manuscript of one gospel would inadvertently, or intentionally, insert words which he remembered as following in another gospel. Mistakes also occur when the copyist changes a word or sentence for what he thinks a better expression. A transcriber at a later date may have two copies of a gospel before him having certain sentences which do not correspond with one another though equally meant to represent the original: he writes down both sentences to make his effort complete, as he thinks. The order of passages may come to be altered in various copies. We have what we may call 'families' of editions of a book which has been often copied and recopied. X, who copied the original, made a few slips. Y copied it and made different slips. Z, others of his own. All the copies made from X's transcription will reproduce X's errors unless the scribe purposely corrects them. So with Y. So with Z. Everyone copying from these descendants of X, or Y, or Z may also make further mistakes. Thus types or classes and 'families' of manuscripts are evolved; there is no pure descent in any family, and there is 'mixture' to be found whenever a manuscript mainly belonging to one group is crossed with a manuscript of another group. This sort of thing being continued leads further and further from the author's own words, especially when, later on, authorized editions or revisions of the copies in circulation were deliberately undertaken. We want to discover what the author himself wrote, neither changed by an oversight nor corrected, nor edited and revised, nor improved or laborated.

There is a game in which one person starts by whispering a short story to someone sitting next to him, who passes it on, whispering it to the next person; this person to the next and so on. When the first to start the story and the last to hear it compare notes, the original story will have been curiously transformed! A similar kind of fate may befall a manuscript which has been copied and copied and passed down the ages.

The mere number of the manuscripts giving a certain form of the words counts for very little. The work of our friend X may have been copied a hundred times, the work of Y twice only: but, if Y, in the first instance, more accurately copied the words of the original than X did, the two descendants of Y give a better indication of what the author wrote than do the hundred who represent X. The antiquity of a manuscript, it will be noted, does not necessarily enhance its value: but it naturally affords some presumption that a manuscript

Apostles, and in that book St. Luke's correctness and care can
traced even more fully than in his Gospel. The period covered
the Acts, comprising the movements of the Apostles, and especial
of St. Paul, offers many points of history, geography and Rom
government in regard to which a careless writer would frequent
have gone astray.

If St. Luke saw the great importance of certainty we may consid
how many there are at the present time to whom certainty in rega
to divine realities would be extremely precious. But they find
many capable people who regard certainty as unobtainable that th
wonder whether they ought to commit themselves. They would
wise to consider whether those who speak against the possibility
certainty being achieved are really satisfactory guides, for one secti
of such persons is led, I fear, by the notion that it is broadminded
regard everything as an open question; but as a matter of fact th
inability to reach a decision may really be a sign of weakness.
cannot defer to it.

And these hesitating folk have to remember that in our relatio
to other people and in our knowledge of them, whether they are o
contemporaries or belong to a past age, and equally in our appr
hension of God, we can never look for a mathematical demonstratic
or for the kind of assurance which comes from experiments in physic
science. Many make this mistake; but, however widespread it ma
be, we cannot surrender to this tendency, this *zeitgeist*, withou
thinking for ourselves. We rightly judge our friend's attitude towar
us and of his affection for us by his bearing and conduct to us: w
cannot see into his heart, but by the indications which meet our ey
we reach certainty.

Again we are not *compelled* to believe in the things which St. Lu
or St. Paul has taught us about God. We have a free will of o
own; and one of the temptations which was put before Our Lord,
St. Luke tells us, was that He should work such a miracle as wou
compel men to believe in Him.

If we turn to the history of a past age we do not expect to fi
such certainty as arises in the case of a scientific demonstration. W
cannot have a past event repeated before our eyes so that we ma
form our judgment upon it, but we can reach 'certainty' in St. Luke
sense by considering the documents referring to the event and th
credibility of those who have recorded the things that happened an
the coherence of the story. Theophilus must have done this.

There are many who are deterred from believing in God's love an
care by the thought of their own insignificance, but the very peop
who have taught us how small we are individually in compariso

th the whole race of mankind have also taught us how small is the
rld in which we live. They cannot overwhelm us by contrasting
with it. Size is not the dominant factor. What broken heart
uld be comforted in a personal bereavement by the gift of a
untain? Value comes before size, and the biggest things are not
e most important. How many there are who instinctively, by a
gic of the soul, recognize the grandeur and the supreme cogency of
r Lord's reasoning: "Are not two sparrows sold for a farthing and
e of them shall not fall on the ground without your Father. . . .
ar ye not therefore, ye are of more value than many sparrows."
e need not discredit this intuition or hesitate to follow. Our friends
o desire to feel 'certain' and dare not, must remember that these
archings about God do not raise solely mental questions: our
ole personality comes into the matter. "If any man will ($\theta\epsilon\lambda\epsilon\iota$)
the will of God, he shall know of the doctrine whether it be of
d." Mind and will and emotion, all three together take part in
e search "To do the will of God", They are mistaken guides who
nore the fact that all that is really good comes from God. We
ay not hide God behind goodness. And some of us go a step farther
d find a Christian foundation for what is best in our civilization
d culture. We cannot cut off our noblest aspirations and achieve-
ents from Christ's teaching. It has coloured and lifted up the best
andards of humanity for many who disclaim any allegiance to
rist, but without being aware of it, have indirectly learnt from
im or from His disciples. The Christian does not believe that we
n keep fresh these standards without again and again referring to
e Life and Person and Teaching of Christ. We cannot rely on
ristian ways and influences continuing of themselves. Human
ogress will not run forward if we leave God out. If we did not know
is before, have we not learnt it from our enemies in this present
nflict, which is at the bottom a spiritual warfare?

There are people who enjoy their difficulties and would be sorry if
ey were removed by their attaining to certainty. Sometimes they
mind me of a woman on Waterloo Bridge. When I was young there
as a halfpenny toll for crossing it. One day my father was delayed
/ an altercation between the toll-keeper and a woman who main-
ined that she had been paid for by a group of friends who were in
ont of her. The discussion was becoming protracted and my father
ing in a hurry put down a penny, saying, "I pay for this lady."
The toll-keeper was of course quite satisfied and the argument
opped, but to the great disgust of the woman, who so much enjoyed
e dispute and the doubt, that she was vexed at being deprived of
em. We are not likely to learn much from the doubters by choice.

We cannot expect to see or measure every reality. God shows
quite enough to create certainty in the minds of those who are rea
to think and do not ask for some short cut which will relieve them
their own responsibility. What He makes plain now brings the prom
of something fuller in the eternal world. "Now we see through
glass darkly." Looking into the mirror that we have in our ha
is not the same as seeing the reality itself, but the mirror gives
reflection of something real, it does not provide an imaginary pictu
even though our limited faculties do not yet see the whole face to fa
We may be content if we can see God as Christ has revealed Hi
Christ leaves no sense of uncertainty. He has, in His human li
brought the Eternal before the eyes of men and by His prese
with us through the Holy Spirit, He does, perhaps specially in
Holy Communion, the very same still for ourselves. If we fol
where He leads, we need not be disturbed if we have to leave so
things over; there is much that is beyond us now, but what we do
know cannot rob us of the certainty of what we do know. When
have the certainty of those things in which we have been instruct
we will be prepared to wait for the full light to show us more. We n
be like the poor afflicted relations whom, after a great colliery disas
in Durham, Bishop Moule went to comfort with the thought of Go
love. He followed up his words by showing to them the back of
embroidered marker in his Bible made by his mother. All that th
could see was a meaningless mass of stitches. Then he turned it o
and it revealed the text on the front: 'God is love.' If we have
certainty of God's love in our hearts we can, in the perplexities th
remain, be ready to wait to see the other side. 'God is His o
interpreter, and He will make it plain.'

The story of St. Thomas the doubter is full of warning and
hope. He declared to the ten believing disciples that he would
believe, unless his test of the reality of the Lord's resurrection v
satisfied by his seeing in Christ's hands the print of the nails, and
thrusting his hand into His side. What would this have prove
Only that the dead body had come to life again like the body
Lazarus. This he did learn for sure; but he learnt much more th
that, when he came into the presence of the Risen Christ who, if
had only been restored as Lazarus was, would have died later a seco
time: the highest hopes of St. Thomas would have been destroy
But when he behold his Lord, Thomas, rising far above his own te
exclaimed: "My Lord and My God." The other disciples had
expelled the sceptic from their company, nor had he cut himself
from them, and Thomas, surrounded by this fellowship, uttered
fullest recognition of the Risen Lord that had as yet been spok

they all heard the Lord pronounce the last beatitude of the pel: "Blessed are they which have not seen and yet have believed." e are three grand certainties: Thomas was certain, and all those since his day have believed without seeing have found the same ainty, and this blessing is certain for them. And now we must a little further across the narrow stream of death, into the life come, which we have already mentioned. Here we are dealing h a phase of existence with which we can have no familiarity. cannot picture in any detail the future life in which there will neither time nor space. St. Luke alludes to it when he quotes Lord's words to the penitent thief; assuring him that he would alive after death and able to recognize the Lord. If anyone says t the Lord did not remain with the thief in Paradise, this does discredit the faculty of consciousness and self-awareness of ich the Lord spoke with certainty. And we remember that St. ke was the companion of St. Paul, the pages of his gospel show ething of the influence of St. Paul in their large-hearted, universal eal. St. Paul, writing to Philippi—which was very likely St. ke's own city—says that he considered it very far better to depart l to be with Christ, Who had now ascended into Heaven. St. Luke st have been familiar with such teaching of Paul, which is full of tainty.

Our thoughts about the world to come cannot be clear cut; but y need not be uncertain. We are wiser to accept the lead given us many hymns, children's hymns and others, than to turn to scientific philosophical discussions which on this subject by the nature of case cannot reach precision. The children's hymns are not of rse descriptions, but when we think of the life to come they express truth in a symbolic fashion and bring out the reality and certainty phrases that we can grasp.

> There is a happy land, far, far away,
> Where saints in glory stand, bright, bright as day;
> Oh we shall happy be, when from sin and sorrow free,
> Lord we shall reign with Thee,
>   Reign, reign for aye.

Only a picture! Yes: but the children are certain about it, and do well to follow them, and so to find a focus for our thoughts and pirations.

It is quite irrelevant for any to denounce here as a grave mistake e notion that the world has, as it were, three levels: Heaven above, e earth on which we stand, and some lower world into which it is impossible to descend. No doubt real difficulty would arise if using such language we took it literally and forgot that any refere to the world above or below is symbolic, and that we only use s terms in order to give some clear points on which our affections a imaginations can dwell. Vagueness will not help. The same Chr who sometimes unites the two worlds by showing Himself to His c at the time of their death, is Lord of both the dead and the livi He is there in the world to come and Him we know: Jesus Chris the same yesterday and to-day and for ever. *"Heaven's morning bre and earth's vain shadows flee, In life, in death, O Lord, abide with m*

CHAPTER XXIX

Church and People

I AM ONE of the few bishops still living who was present in the Ho of Lords and spoke in the debate with reference to the Enabling A which established the National Assembly of the Church of Engla: I entertained misgivings about it, and can vividly recall the way which Archbishop Davidson, flushed and nervous after the spee in opposition made by Bishop Knox, hurried into the bishops' ro where I was seated correcting some proofs. He said that he had hea that I was going to speak against the Bill, and added that if it c not pass he would have to resign the Archbishopric. I said I did i see the good of such an intention, and I could not myself enter into excitement. In due course, when I did speak in the House, I limit my remarks to indicating certain points which in my opinion I thoug should be adjusted. I then learnt what I have never since forgotte that those who from the first ask for adjustments do not carry mu weight, and that an out-and-out opposition at the beginning is far mc effective, though, of course, as the time goes on, there is the opportuni to suggest modifications. The whole matter of the erection of t Church Assembly has had so great an effect on the Church of Engla: that it will be well to make some general remarks upon the Chur and the people before describing exactly the constitution of t Church Assembly.

It is said, and with truth, that there is a rift between the Chur and the people. This has long been the case in other Europe

ntries, but in England we enjoyed the unique position and privilege
a National Church, with the Church and the people being at one.
course there is always a rift between the ideals of the Church and
practice and habits of the people, but that need not mean a differ-
e of aim and a division of heart. It is frequently alleged that comfort
o be found in the fact that the persons who now do identify them-
ves with the Church are more earnest than in days gone by. But
en we restrict our consideration to those who do frequent church
vices, we cannot be at all sure that we have here only a gain to
ord. There is something in the habit of church-going, for whatever
1se, that is valuable. Even if it is a mere habit without much devo-
n in it, and even if it is, or was, only the way of persons who have
pected the practice of their employers and go to church with some
1se of compulsion, we must remember that if the habit is firmly
ablished it is easier to change it into real devotion than to start
: habit outside the walls of the church. Church-going is in this
pect like private prayer; if the practice of private prayer remains
broken, not only does the discipline of it remain, but one day it can
lighted up with a flame of sincerity.

This regrettable rift shows itself on both sides. On the one side
: Church has become too much interested in itself: it is true that it
es eagerly and successfully come out into the world to help the
rld and improve it, but it is a coming-out from a self-conscious
sition. We see a certain professional attitude among the clergy
d many of them may be primarily interested in organization and
ganizations and ceremonial. The revival of Convocation after a
ose of more than a hundred years has emphasized this attitude of
: clergy. When Convocation was restored to its proper position
took some time for it to grow into its strength; at first it had not
rnt to be effective, and even when Convocation had been re-estab-
hed some of the more important Church questions were dealt with
Parliament and in debates carried on by bishops and others in the
ouse of Lords. The erection of the Church Assembly has also made
: Church more self-centred, for on the parochial Church councils,
:., a line is drawn between the Church of England folk to separate
em from the parishioners at large who have no vote in the new
urch administration if they belong to any denomination outside
: Church of England.

On the other side, the people at large view the Church with some
spicion, and the rift widens. There is more than one reason for this
titude: the spread of an acquaintance with scientific thought seems
make the doctrines of the Church and its teaching old-fashioned
d ill-assorted with the outlook of the modern world. It is not

understood that all truth belongs to the Lord Christ who Himself
the Truth; whether he knows it or does not realize it, every hon
seeker and finder of a truth is working in Christ's Kingdom in allegia
to Him. This supposed discrepancy between science and the Chur
together with the higher criticism of the books of the Bible, has c
credited the Bible in the eyes of many who have forgotten that
Bible is a spiritual library. We turn to it to learn about the thi
of God and about the Lord Christ, who is the Way and the Life
well as the Truth. The Bible was not written in order to teach
facts of history or to provide us with information which we can disco
for ourselves by observation and study. We have it put into c
hands and hearts that we may learn what God Himself has decla
about Himself and about men, their nature and opportunities and t
goal of their life. The Bible is not a book full of puzzles and co
tradictions, it is a revelation, and they are wrong who suppose th
they may turn their backs upon it because it contains pictures
conduct and character that would certainly shock us now, if we
not recognize that the Old Testament was pointing forward to Chr
Himself by whose own teaching many of the things which offe
are superseded.

It cannot be denied that for these or other reasons the Chur
to a great extent stands away from the large national life of the count
Moreover, in many ways, thanks to the influence and example of t
Church, the State has taken over activities which formerly fell with
the province of the Church and sets itself to fulfil them, without nec
sarily relying on any help from the Church: the care of the sick a
poor and suffering, the education of the children and other simi
enterprises have passed from the direct responsibilities of the Chur
into the hands of the State. The Church can still keep a watch
eye upon the way in which the State discharges the new duties whi
it has taken upon itself and the Church can, in many ways, help t
State in these respects. The Parish is in some regards merged into
larger district, and the parish is no longer the one unit, with the pars
leading the way.

We are told that less leadership is found among the bishops th
used to be the case. This is partly due to the way in which the numb
of bishops has been augmented. This increase was intended to promo
diocesan efficiency; but, strangely enough, all the time diocese
vigour has been restricted by the developments of the Church Assemb
while the independence of individual bishops has been limited by t
centralization of Church government in London, and so has t
independence of the parish priest. We often hear in public life of t
drawbacks which attend upon too large a Cabinet, and now that the

e more than forty diocesan bishops we suffer from the same kind
thing in the Church. The bishops have come to be more of a board
an a brotherhood, and one who becomes a member of a board is more
an likely to follow the regulations of the board and its tendencies than
take any free line of action. There is no shortage of able men fit
r promotion in the hierarchy of the Church, but it is a dangerous
ing for a man to lose his own independence and to be content to
llow the prevalent official tradition.

It is stated that four-fifths of the area of England is placed in
untry parishes, and that four-fifths of the population is aggregated
towns. When we discuss the position or the relation between the
urch and the people we have to bear this in mind. In the great
wns it is not possible for the clergy to be on intimate terms with the
ousands of their parishioners, and it is very difficult to estimate the
inions and the attitude of the people. So far as attendance in church
es, the few who go to church have a large choice of churches within
ach of them. In the villages it is different, where the life is much
ore intimate; but the spread of Anglo-Catholic ways does not make
the towns the great difference it does in one-church areas in rural
ngland. Speaking generally we may say that with some few notable
d splendid exceptions many of the Anglo-Catholic clergy, with their
ll ceremonial and exclusively sacramental requirements, have not
mmended themselves to their parishioners. The congregation does
t like the artificial clerical voice. Many also are against the constant
e of confession, and consider that it intrudes into domestic intimacies
d comes between the members of a family. The Prayer Book
ems to provide it as a medicine and not as a food, though I have
ard a prominent ecclesiastic occupying a position of authority
y that its words: "God hath given power and commandment to His
inisters to declare and pronounce to His people, being penitent, the
bsolution and Remission of their sins", enjoins the hearing of indivi-
al confessions. (He was not referring to the stronger, but conditional
ords in the Visitation of the Sick.) Others take the words to refer to
hat follows on, about the Holy Gospel's general declaration of God's
rdon for the truly penitent.

We can scarcely follow the lead of those who maintain that the
ccess of the Church is bound up with the Oxford Movement, which
fers an easier outward satisfaction through the due, if sometimes
ly formal, observance of rites and rules; the heart's devotion matters
ore. Such critics urge that the clergy in the Evangelical days, which
llowed upon the rousing call of Wesley and his colleagues, found their
rength in promoting the personal devotion of individual upright
d saintly lives. Was not this a great achievement and would not

many people be very glad to watch the spread of this kind of goodn‹
now? It does not betoken stagnation, and many of the habits n‹
rather scornfully characterized as items in Victorian respectabili‹
would be worth very much in our own generation. Certainly no c
who looks to Rome for inspiration will carry the bulk of Engli
people with him; it is only as individuals that any lean that wa
Anyhow, we do not wish to see the Church adopting such a positi‹
as will put aside whole ranges of good conduct and character a‹
believing in only one style of churchmanship that cannot be said ‹
be altogether successful. Lecky has written: "It is difficult to belie‹
that serious dangers do not await the Church if the unprotestantizi‹
influences that are spread within it continue to extend. It is r
likely that the nation will continue to give its support to the Chur‹
if that Church and its main tendencies cuts itself off from t‹
Reformation.

"If the Church of England becomes in general what it already‹
in some of its churches, it is not likely that English public opini‹
will permanently acquiesce in its privileged position in the Sta‹
If it ceases to be a Protestant Church, it will not long remain ‹
established one, and its disestablishment would probably be follow‹
by a disruption in which opinions would be more sharply defined a‹
the latitude of belief and the spirit of compromise that now character‹
our English religious life might be seriously impaired."

Through many centuries now there have been two currents ‹
the Church of England. At one time the bishops and the clergy ha‹
laid stress upon the Catholic tradition; at another on the Evangeli‹
outlook, though we must note that the position of the Pope and t‹
ban on clerical marriage will always prevent the former group ‹
clergy from turning as a body to Rome. Roman clergy who wi‹
to minister in the Church of England sometimes approve the Chur‹
of England's preference for married clergy. But it would be a mista‹
for either section to try to exclude the other. Their respective phi‹
sophies of life make it easier for the Anglo-Catholics to make a pub‹
impression than for the Evangelicals to do so. The former put t‹
corporate life of the Church first and co-operate better; the latt‹
put first the individual's relation to God in Christ, so that there ‹
less coherence among them, and however great is their influen‹
they make a less concentrated effect. But in the whole truth the‹
two philosophies do not contradict one another. One of the m‹
common sources of friction in political and administrative life ‹
found in views and aims and schemes which are really supplementa‹
to one another being regarded as opposed.

History will show us what I do not propose to try to elabora‹

QUEEN MARY ON HER WAY TO LAYING THE FOUNDATION STONE OF ST. CATHERINE'S CHURCH,
MILE CROSS, 1935

The Archdeacon of Norfolk, the Bishop of Norwich, Queen Mary, the Chief Constable of Norwich, Mr. Gerald Chichester,
Lady Victoria Forrester.

THE PALACE FROM THE EAST

e, that in the last century and a half there has been in the Church
England a kind of oscillation between the two ways of devotion,
 Anglo-Catholic and the Evangelical. This is unfortunate; it
uld have been better if each had heartily respected the other
thout desire to predominate, and if both could have cordially amal-
mated without rivalry or mutual contempt, and made allowances
 diversities of religious and emotional temperament.

When the Christian basis of all that is best in our civilization
d conduct is being assaulted, is it too late for us in our generation
 seek such concord now, while we all carefully exclude any extrava-
nces to which neither the Bible nor the Prayer Book gives sanction?
r this fraternal combination is the way of the Prayer Book, with
 insistence on both the Word and the Sacraments. But such
mbination or amalgamation must be founded on a sound mutual
;ard and not on a lip service of brotherliness that is liable to break
wn when some strain occurs, in the way in which, with all our
erances about our growing fellowship, the Church of England
d the Free Churches cannot at present really disguise the division
tween them. This allusion to the Free Churches leads on to a
al remark that though this chapter has primarily been concerned
:h the Church of England, no one could close his eyes to the valuable
itribution made by the Free Churches to English devotion and
aracter. We need it at this juncture; this time of challenge; and
ne of the points made in this article concern us all.

CHAPTER XXX

he National Assembly of the Church of England

E CHURCH ASSEMBLY was set up in the year 1919. The main cause
 its erection was the difficulty of getting Church legislation through
rliament. In Archbishop Benson's *Life* we read of his disappoint-
nts in this direction. Parliament had, and has, too much work
 hand to give adequate consideration to sectional matters. One
ist not, however, exaggerate, for in the years just before the Church
sembly came into existence a very important Act was passed through
rliament to replace the cumbrous procedure previously in use for
iting parishes together. Lord Birkenhead was of great assistance

E

in this matter. The plans for uniting benefices have been revi
more than once, but this Act may be said to stand at the foundat
of them. The Church Assembly has now been long enough in existe
for it to be possible to weigh up some of its results.

Putting it very shortly, one may say that the Church Assem
consists of three Houses, the Diocesan Bishops constitute one of the
the Representatives elected by the clergy, styled Proctors, make
second House; and the House of Laity, elected, like the Proctors,
the Dioceses, makes the third House. These lay representatives
not chosen in exactly the same way by every Diocese, but all who
elected must be communicants of the Church of England. The vot
in each parish consist of those who are eighteen years old and
members of the Church of England and do not belong to any ot
denomination.

It can at once be seen that this sytem tends, as I have remark
to divide up the people of a parish. It draws a definite line betw
those who do, and those who do not, belong to the Church of Engla
"So much the better," say some persons, among whom are to be fou
those who would prefer that only communicants should be entitled
vote. In every parish there is a parochial church council to wh
definite powers have been assigned, but those who do not belong
the Church of England are excluded from their activities. In
parishes an affection for the parish church—and in many cases
the services in it—is held by those who belong to one or anothe
the Free Churches. It has often been a practice in the country
people to attend service in the church at one time of the day and a
free church chapel at another. But the Church Assembly and
subordinate councils, though not forbidding such a practice, has mar
it with a stamp of irregularity or, at any rate, cut off the Church
England much more strictly from other Christian bodies, even tho
their members may be baptised.

There are elaborate rules for the procedure in the work of
Assembly, some of them dealing with the various stages befor
Measure is passed. When in the end a Measure has been so pas
and has received the Royal Assent it has the validity of an Act
Parliament. It would be tedious here to detail these rules or to sp
of the relation in the Assembly between the House of Bishops and
House of Clergy and the House of Laity. When the Assembly
passed a Measure it goes before a body termed the Ecclesiast
Committee, nominated by the Lord Chancellor and the Speaker of
House of Commons, which reports to Parliament on the nature
every Measure and states whether it regards the Measure in quest
as expedient, especially with relation to the constitutional right

Majesty's subjects. A Measure does not go straight from the
embly to the Ecclesiastical Committee, but passes through the
ds of a Parliamentary Committee of the Church Assembly. The
liamentary Committee of the Church Assembly can approach the
lesiastical Committee and consider the attitude of the Ecclesiastical
nmittee and the draft of its proposed Report to Parliament and
ide whether to go forward in the matter; if necessary the Parlia-
ntary Committee can then go back to the Assembly for a further
sideration. Neither the Ecclesiastical Committee nor Parliament
lf can amend a proposed Measure in any way. This does not pretend
be an exhaustive and precise account of the methods by which
Church Assembly and the subordinate bodies concerned with it
k, but it gives the general outline of this great revolution in
rch government.

Some excellent achievements stand to the credit of the Church
embly and we may specially give as an illustration the Dilapida-
s Measure passed in 1923. The Dilapidations in parsonage houses
long caused much trouble and many of the clergy had evaded their
igations. The Measure has put the whole subject on to a firm and
inesslike footing. One of the best speeches ever made in the
rch Assembly was the extremely lucid speech in which Bishop
ittingham expounded its fifty-three clauses, most of which had
ny sub-sections. The Clergy Pensions Measure, again, has also
ed for much attention from the Assembly. It is difficult to see
time could have been found in Parliament for considering these
plicated matters.

At the same time it must be confessed that neither the House of
rgy nor the House of Laity is really representative of those for
om they speak. There is much piety and purpose outside the
use of Laity to be found among those who have not yet thrown
mselves into the new system. As the years go by the Assembly
y be better appreciated. But Englishmen are reticent in regard
their deepest feelings and do not find it easy in religious matters
come forward as candidates or to use the votes to which they are
itled. The election of Members of Parliament no doubt leaves
ch to be desired and the number of voters who vote is regrettably
ll, but the case is worse still in these Church elections. Moreover,
ther the Proctors nor the Lay representatives have easy access to
ir 'constituents'. The sittings of the Assembly take place only
ee times in a year, and of course proposals put before it can be
y much modified in the actual discussions. Outside the Assembly
s very difficult for the clergy and laity to follow the proceedings
to adjust their views to meet the various stages that are reached.

There is no money for expenses, and it is hard for a representativ‹
keep those whom he represents up to date with what is going
No plan has yet been devised for reaching the real opinion of the cl‹
at large, and of laymen in general, who may only wake up to w
is being done, or has been done, when it is too late to alter it. At
other end, the proceedings in Parliament have tended to become for
and perfunctory. It is the old story over again; Parliament can ra
spare the time to debate a report from the Ecclesiastical Commit
At the time of the proposed revision of the Prayer Book the w‹
country was stirred and time was given for considering the ma
in both Houses of Parliament. But, generally speaking, the re‹
of the Ecclesiastical Committee is accepted and endorsed. I
doubtful whether this was anticipated at the beginning. In
respect the Enabling Act, as it was called, under which these g‹
changes took place, has been a disappointment. Archbishop Davi‹
more than once made it plain that it was by no wish of his that Pa‹
ment stood aside in this way. When Parliament did interpose in
issue of the Prayer Book revision, many churchmen thought ‹
even though it was acting strictly in accordance with the rights gi
to it in the scheme which was initiated by the Church itself, it ha‹
business to interfere with spiritual matters or that only Eng
churchmen should have voted. It has not, however, been the wa‹
Parliament to divide itself up into sections, so that, for exam‹
only those concerned with a district asking for some local rearra‹
ment should be allowed to exercise their right to vote. Parliam
is not a miscellany of unrelated fractions but deals as a whole ‹
any matter brought up for its consideration. It is far away from
truth to say that in rejecting the revised Prayer Book Parliam‹
was dictating its doctrines to the Church. Parliament has no p‹
but that of veto, and in exercising its veto it has to consider
theological niceties but what it believes to be for the general wel
of the nation. There are many who hold the opinion that Parliam‹
on this occasion better interpreted the devout will and feeling of
nation than the Church Assemblies had.

Speaking generally, it is doubtful whether the parochial ch‹
councils, especially in the country districts, can exercise satisfact‹
the powers given to them. They may not know enough about
subject with which they try to deal; for example, they are not s
ciently acquainted with the possibilities of church and clerical lif
exercise helpfully such power as they now have in the choice of a
clergyman for their own parish. One must not generalize too wi‹
but often they are unaware how limited is the choice of men who
be willing to accept a particular post. They chiefly or only know‹

gy living close by. It needs much care to get together a satis-
.ory Church council; there may not be enough candidates and the
.tion between the council and the clergyman in a small parish may
ve unsatisfactory, not least so when it is practically filled by his
ninating those connected with his own household. It is difficult
England to prophesy how a new institution will work. The County
ncils have been a great success and, generally speaking, they
·e admirably handled the various sections of all the work assigned
them; but parish councils have not answered equally well. It is
then surprising that some parts of this new method of Church
·ernment have been more successful than others. The National
irch as an institution has a very long past behind it in the life of
gland. Many ways and habits and affections have grown up round
irough the centuries. Respect, strong and deep-rooted, for example,
ongs to the office of churchwarden, not abolished, but in some
)ects modified by the new scheme. No wonder if it needs time for
irch folk and others in the parishes to take into their heads and
·rts the new plans which have been made for them, some indeed, in a
iewhat academic style, differing from their age-long ways. In
towns the Church Councils are more successful.

The position of the Archbishop of Canterbury in the Church
embly is anomalous. He presides over its deliberations and is
)onsible for the conduct of the business; but, like any other bishop,
has the right to speak, and he can influence—which often means
trol—the vote. Archbishop Davidson may be said to have made
Assembly work, and in some respects the Assembly made him.
·e Archbishop may be put into a false position if he has to commend
the House of Lords a Measure to which he is personally opposed.

The level of speaking in the Assembly is high, probably better than
Parliament; but the same speakers appear too frequently on the
tform and tend to become bores: many make their speeches too
ç and are not content to stand aside if the arguments which they
·duce have already been expressed by others. In any deliberative
embly most speakers are thinking not only of the audience they are
iressing but of the account they can give, when they go home, of
mselves and of their contribution. The Assembly is much moved by
ttiment and swayed by feeling. It is not the wisest speakers who
. the applause, and there are certain points mentioned again and
·in of which the Assembly never tires, e.g. over-large parsonage
ises, etc.

It must be confessed that the Church Assembly has taken away
ch of the freedom and spontaneity which belonged to the parishes
l dioceses. Some of the Measures tend to organize Church life too

far and to subject it to a central control. Much that is of value
lost in the process. It is all to the good that ideas should be exchang
and that methods found useful in one direction or locality should
employed in another, but it is a misfortune if liberty has to
surrendered to bureaucratic control.

We shall have to wait for another twenty-five or fifty years befc
a final judgment can be given. The creation of the Assembly seem
to Sir Lewis Dibdin, if I remember right, to point on to the disesta
lishment of the Church, because it seemed to surrender its natio1
character to sectional organization and efficiency. Some to whom
precise Church system is very dear would not object if disestablishme
dominated the future. Others, however, less appreciative of the log
and academic coherence that are foreign to the English mind, reck
that disestablishment, which would put the Church of England on
the same kind of footing as other Christian bodies, would be a disas'
to the nation; "ours is a Christian land," said Archbishop Davidsc
and the National Church is a bulwark of this position. We have be
speaking of the National Assembly of the Church of England. C
we safely ignore the first word of this title?

CHAPTER XXXI

Disestablishment

I HAVE EXPRESSED myself frequently on this subject. After some ye;
of disuse this word appears to be coming to the fore again, but
rather a different way from that in which the question was forme1
raised. In old days there was some animosity against the Church
England on the part of the members of the Free Churches and th
were the prime movers in any effort to disestablish it. Their attitu
has undergone a change. They are now much more inclined to lo
upon the Church of England as the primary bulwark supporti
Christianity in the country. No doubt if the Church of England,
any serious way, changed its forms of worship or its teaching, th
might begin to hold another estimate concerning it. It will be reme
bered that, at the time when the revision of the Prayer Book v
under discussion, they were against the alterations proposed in 1
Book, and were to be found among the supporters of the Church
England, so far as it was pledged to the Book of 1662.

The word 'Disestablishment' is now more used by the internal
ics of the Church of England, or by those who, being members of
are coming to think that it is abandoning its old moorings. The
ter are inclined to say that the Church of England has been changing
character in the last thirty years. I have, before now, mentioned
t a clergyman on whom I much relied once said to me, in view of
ent changes in the policy and the outlook of the Church of England:
his is not the Church into which I was ordained." It is possible
t the Oxford Movement might carry the Church so far in the direc-
n of the Church of Rome that people who share his views might
r that they no longer had a stake in it and that the Church of
gland was no longer worth supporting. Some of them would say:
the Church is disestablished, I should not care."

The people of England are in a unique position in having a national
urch of their own. It is a great heritage which has come down to us
m the past and it would be a mistake lightly to break the bond
ween the Church and the State. Archbishop D'Arcy of Armagh
e wrote:

"Remember that in great countries on the continent of Europe,
t to look to more distant lands, Church and State are more or less
continual conflict, or in a condition of armed neutrality in relation
one another. The Church comes, in such circumstances, to be
arded by great numbers as a vast conspiracy against the liberties
the nation. That is a terrible state of things; and the freedom of
gland from that disastrous condition has been due to the fact that
English people, with their profound common sense, and their
ppy disregard of the abstract doctrines of the theorist, have always
termined to be masters in their own house, and to have their own
tional Church as part of the whole economy of their national life.
e real meaning of the Establishment of the Church of England is
t that. It expresses the Christian Faith of the nation. It is the
tion on the religious side. Some theorists, in order to throw discredit
all this, call it Erastian. Calling names is always a stupid form of
gument. But Erastianism is really not the correct description.
ll it organic, and the relation of Church and State in England becomes
ar. The people of England inherited their Faith and inherited
eir Church as essentials of the national life, and there is no sign that
ey want to part with these great possessions. Recent events seem
prove quite clearly that the people, not merely of England, but of
Great Britain, mean to preserve the Church, and to preserve it
such a way as may make it continue to be the true representative
the Faith of the nation. I understand, of course, that there would
real ground of objection if Parliament attempted to introduce into

the standards of the Church novelties of doctrine or practice.
must be remembered that the State did not, at the Reformation
subsequently, dictate to the Church in matters of doctrine or practi
The Prayer Book in its various forms, as it has come down to mode
times, was the work of the Church accepted by the State; but nev
the work of the Church apart from the approval of the State. It w
ever the task of the Church to initiate, and the task of the State
sanction, that which was presented, or to refuse sanction if
determined."

This does not mean that, apart from any reference to the Fr
Churches, everyone who belongs to the Church of England is co
stantly and sincerely an adherent of it in his practice and habi
But the acknowledgment of God, for which the Church stands,
our public and national life is something very precious. Our Hous
of Parliament day by day open with prayer to God. There is a servi
in connection with every Assize when the Judges go on circuit.
the Church were disestablished Peers and Members of Parliame
could use private prayers if they pleased to do so; Judges, sherif
and members of corporations could pray at home before approachi
their duties. But too many fail to see the distinction between pub
and private prayer. In our access to God, public prayer is not a
accumulation of private prayers; it is something of a different charact
The official work of the nation thus confesses an allegiance to Go
The religious dedication of the Sovereign to his high vocation fou
in our Coronation Service counts for much. Among the people
England and the peoples of the King's dominions beyond the seas
even, one can believe, among men of many creeds—the solemn setti
apart of the British Sovereign and the dedication of him to his suprem
vocation appeals to a religious faith which is something more tha
personal loyalty and affecting sentiment. The Coronation is n
only a religious ceremony but an authoritatively national service.

And the influence of the established Church in England reach
into our Dominions where the Church is not established. It is right
felt that those who follow its ways of worship and its outlook upc
life gain a greater influence upon the welfare of the community
which they live because they are in association with the establishc
Church in England. Abandonment of the public national recognitic
of religion would deal a blow to all religion. Archbishop Frederic
Temple of Canterbury once wrote: "I think Disestablishment will I
a step down for the whole nation." We may go further and say tha
the whole Empire would be affected, even though Christian though
and Christian influence would still radiate from Christian peopl
serving their generation in public and private life. But this is not th

me thing as the avowed recognition of God in the general direction affairs. The Church of England, national and established, by its ry existence utters a protest against the unfortunate tendency to aw a sharp line between the sacred and the secular; it openly mphasizes the truth that all life, public and private, with its manifold portunities, 'stands upon holy ground'.

The ministers of the Church, whether Bishops or Clergy, must ways look upwards to the Lord in Heaven for their primary commission, and one can imagine such a state of things arising as would ake them demand a severance from the State. Some persons now ok at Germany and, viewing what is taking place there, only too ainly see the degradation of what pretends to be a national Church. is conceivable, for the sake of argument, that the same kind of ing might happen in England. But the very fact that the whole ation has, together in service and sacrifice, combined to defeat e anti-Christian outlook of the German people, at least would seem show that neither in Church nor in State have we any leaning wards the policy which the German rulers favour in regard to conduct professed worship.

The Church of England was not established by any Act of Parliament; its disestablishment could not be accomplished by the repeal some existing Act. Acts of Parliament no doubt have been passed facilitate a change in the position of those who wish formally to ssociate themselves from the Church; and the number of persons ho take no interest in religion or decline to identify themselves with e Church's Christian affirmations has much increased and has duced the solidity and solidarity of the Church from the days when tizen and churchman were, so to speak, interchangeable terms. nd we all know that while Parliament has the last say in legislation r the Church of England, the House of Commons is elected by voters ho are not required to possess any religious qualifications, and the embers of it and of the House of Lords need have no religious beliefs. evertheless, our standards are Christian standards; and a national cognition of God is still found in the very existence of the Church England dating right away from the earliest times: the laws of ing Alfred begin with a recital of the Ten Commandments. This osition cannot be altered except by definite legislation to that effect. or here a point which is often missed must be emphasized—namely, at it is rather for the nation than for the Church to choose whether stablishment is wanted. The Church as a spiritual body could refuse be attached to the State in any way, and could desire some way of verance; but if the Church is ready to serve the State in the present osition, it is for the nation to decide whether it welcomes its services.

E*

Bishop Burge, of Oxford, once said half-humorously to me: "If t
nation really knew the value to itself of all that an established Chur
brings, it would say to the Church: 'In no case will we allow you
be disestablished, not even if you propose it yourself.' "

The coherence of the Church of England is, to a large extent, d
to its comprehensive character, which the establishment safeguarc
No one party can dominate the whole situation. I suppose that if t
Church were disestablished, one result might be that the differe
sections which now live together in it might each form a separa
organization living apart from the others. The width and the toleran
which at present the Church exhibits would perish in the formatic
of separate bodies. And the rules of each body would be more rigid
drawn up and more rigidly imposed: the Law would protect and enfor
any pledges and undertakings and forms of contract involved. I
man and no society of men can be wholly exempt from the control
the State.

There are those who are asking that the Church of England shou
be put into the position held by the Church of Scotland. To tl
suggestion it may be replied that the whole history of the two countri
is so different as to make the proposal irrelevant. It may be enough
quote some words from *The History of England*, by the Master
Trinity, Mr. George Trevelyan, O.M.:

"The divergent courses which the Reformation had followed
England and in Scotland respectively did much to complicate t
politics of the succeeding era, when the rule of a single King over bo
countries constantly pointed towards ecclesiastical union that was,
fact, always impossible.

"At the Reformation the laity on both sides of the Border h
asserted their will against the mediæval clergy, but in two very d
ferent ways. In England the Church had kept the outline of its ancie
organization, remaining purely clerical in its structure; it follow
that the control of the laity over its liturgy and doctrine had to
exercised not from within but from without, through Crown ai
through Parliament. In Scotland, on the other hand, the laity to
an active part in Church organization and government. Only
could there be any control of religion by the laity, because they h
no real Parliament to speak for them.

"The Church Assembly has not yet filled the gap."

We do not wish to think too much of the privileges which
connection with the State, as is sometimes argued, confers upon t
Church of England. The chief advantage which the clergy enjoy
the security of their position; that is to say, they are protected fro
any tyrannical interference on the part of those who are set over the

d they are not at the mercy of those to whom they minister. In
ssing it should be noted that this independence has to some extent
en altered by recent legislation.

If you ask an ordinary, well-informed but thoughtless person
hat is meant by the establishment of the Church of England, you
ill probably find that in most cases he will answer that it means that
e bishops have seats in the House of Lords. But not all the bishops
ve seats, and I do not know that it could be urged that those who
ve not yet reached a place in the House of Lords have their spiritual
ork impaired by this fact. No doubt it is a great advantage in all
gislation that the bishops can make their voices heard on the moral
sues involved, and though the bishops who sit in the House have
ecial and direct opportunities, the formation of a wholesome public
inion does not exclusively depend upon these particular bishops, and
ere are many who can do this altogether outside the House of Lords.

But the loftiest privilege of the bishops and clergy is to be found
their special opportunities of advancing the welfare of the people
d promoting the extension of the Kingdom of God among men
rough their ministrations in church and outside the church. It
nnot be denied that this is no longer the ideal of all the clergy. Some
w lay all the stress upon the church services and draw aside from
e people, as if they themselves belonged to a priestly caste. The
eat importance of parochial visiting is less recognized. Be that as
may, there is one clergyman resident among his flock in every
rish—or pair of parishes—to whom the people entrusted to his
arge may of right turn for help. He can dedicate himself wholly
strengthening and sweetening every bit of their lives by God's grace.
ow many of them do this? His interest is not withheld from the
ee Church folk in the parish. It is one of the great advantages of
e Church of England maintaining a married clergy that the home
the clergyman stands among the homes of his parishioners. In
is regard it is easier for the country parson to know his people
dividually and intimately, though rural parishes require some
justments and adaptations owing to the movement of so many
om the countryside to the towns. But the principle of the scheme
that a clergyman is the servant of his parish and practically no one
left outside the Church's care. The Free Church men worship by
ngregations and the ministers principally devote themselves to the
embers of the congregation with their families: the clergyman of
e Church of England has committed to him the care of the souls
the whole number of the parishioners. Here is his privilege. Here
his opportunity.

Do not leave out of account the disendowment that would neces-

sarily attend upon disestablishment which would still be spiritua
far the greater disaster. But disendowment would also carry with
the spiritual misfortune of leaving to the disestablished Chur
reduced emoluments with which to continue its work for God. A
what about the churches and the parsonages? Would they be l
in the possession and under the control of the disestablished Churc
or would some scheme of sharing them with or apportioning the
among various denominations be evolved? It is possible that
considerable part of the income and possessions of the Church mig
be diverted from ecclesiastical ownership to humanitarian purpos
Our social services are very costly and in the near future may beco
more costly still. The property of the Church would be ready to har
proposals might be made by those who prefer material to religic
ends, and set no value on the Church's ministrations and activities,
employ its property for useful and charitable objects. They wou
say that the interests of the community would be better served
the diversion of Church endowments to existing or fresh social schem
Much new money could be spent on education, training of youth, t
improvement of the position of the unemployed and the aged, up
the care of the sick and many other good causes. It needs mu
consideration and foresight to recognize all that disendowment mig
involve. It is not to be approached with vague uncertainty of opini
The consequences of both disestablishment and disendowment are
present too loosely apprehended.

There are members of the Church of England who regard th
position in our national Church as putting a bar in the way of th
cohesion with the great Roman Church of the West. Such pers
would deplore the results of the controversies with Rome in t
sixteenth century, and would like to get back behind that period
settlement—or unsettlement. These views, it can scarcely be doubt
are stronger among a certain group of the clergy than among Engl
churchmen in general, or among the Christian community at lar
who reject and deplore anything approaching such an attitude.
is more than doubtful whether any section of the clergy looki
outside England for their spiritual loyalty would carry the wh
Church of England or the nation with them.

It will be a sad day if ever the nation repudiates the Church,
the Church ignores the nation and prefers to revolve round its
Unless they are provoked into a contrary view, Churchmen, Christi
men, Englishmen, will, in all probability, still consider that the Chur
and the nation can do far better together than apart, and that
divorce of one from the other would, in the long run, be harmful
both parties in this union.

CHAPTER XXXII

House of Lords

HEN THE PARLIAMENT ACT (commonly known as the Veto Bill) was ssed at the beginning of the reign of George V, some persons supsed that it deprived the House of Lords of all authority. It is no ubt the case that many would agree with the opinion of Lord avidson, as explained in his *Life*, that it was improper that the King ould have been directly approached in the matter; it would have en better that any proposal should have been set out in a careful emorandum and left for his consideration. Moreover, it is not nerally the English way to deal with constitutional questions in is fashion. We do not, like the Americans, welcome a written nstitution requiring judicial consideration as new points arise. ings in England for the most grow and develop as needs require: example, the system of Cabinet responsibility simply *came*. But e work done by the House of Lords with its new limitations is all portant. It possesses the time and the ability to improve and rify the terms of a Bill sent up from the House of Commons. Still re important is it that the discussions take place in a calm atmohere where many independent Peers can make a contribution to e common cause without political partisanship.

The House of Lords often shows itself as the home of reflective nsideration and balanced judgment.

The gift of judgment is not a popular gift; it seems to lack the thusiasm evoked by partisanship; but if at the time of its exercise receives no ovation, a double reward is given to it when others turn ain and again to its possessor and quietly ask for his help, and when er it is honoured in the retrospect. The man of judgment is unlike e enthusiastic party man who falls into the error of seeing half and t the whole of a matter, and acts as if it were always true that έον ἥμιουπαητός ('the half is greater than the whole')'

Unnecessary controversies will arise because it is often the case at more than one cause contributes to some effect or influences some ue which is under discussion. One set of people is so sure in attriting the result to one reason, and another set so sure in attributing to another reason that they cannot pull together in any effort to prove the situation which confronts them, or find a remedy for a ing which both agree ought to be rectified. The House of Lords n often give a wise lead and reconcile differences.

We can easily think of examples. Some attribute the falli[ng] birth-rate to economic causes: people cannot afford to have childre[n] others attribute it to the avoidance of parental responsibility; a[nd] yet others say that the cause of it is an interference with Nature. The[re] may be truth in each of these opinions, and if people do not spend the time in pressing their own view against that of others, they mig[ht] join hands and work together for the removal of a position which the[y] are all deploring.

Lately, and always, two sides are taken in the matter of educati[on.] One set of people will say that the humane subjects are those [of] primary importance, that a knowledge of philosophy or history, of t[he] arts and of the classics must come first; others wish to clear the fie[ld] in order that science or technical training may have full sway. It [is] perfectly true that there is not time for an intelligent young pers[on] to learn everything. No doubt we should all be learning througho[ut] our lives, but we have to concentrate upon some curriculum an[d] courses of study in early years. In a well-balanced education the[re] will be room for both these two main subjects, for the humaniti[es] and for scientific or technical study: we need the blend.

Professor Salisbury wrote in *The Times*: "One of the chief defec[ts] in our present educational system both in schools and in universiti[es] is that the division of knowledge into subjects, however necessa[ry] as a practical convenience, has led far too often to their treatme[nt] as independent entities so that their relation to one another is lo[st] sight of, and the student fails to apprehend that the separate subje[cts] are but different facets of the same jewel of knowledge. Thus it [is] that the arts and science, alike essential to a liberal education, [so] often fail to become an integrated whole and so contribute as the[y] should to the fuller enjoyment and zest of life."

Mr. G. M. Young has written forcibly on the need of training an[d] forming *intellectual character*. Allowance must be made for the differe[nt] tastes and interests of pupils, but it would be a misfortune if the[ir] leanings were allowed to lead them to specialize in one direction witho[ut] any acquaintance at all with subjects outside the range of it, or if the[y] failed to secure the educational advantage derived through discussi[on] with their contemporaries and seniors of matters of general interes[t.]

Recently we have found that the controversy between day schoo[ls] and boarding schools has been revived. The arguments are familia[r.] Day schools are considered to keep the 'spell of home affection' stro[ng] and sweet. Boarding schools are thought to develop an early sen[se] of corporate life in the citizens of the future. In the former schoo[l] it is urged that time is wasted in travelling, and that it is difficult [to] get in the home circle the quiet space necessary for study and wor[k]

d that the pupil's personality is drawn in two alternating directions.
n the other hand, it is maintained that however good are the results
chieved by the pupils in boarding schools, it is unnatural that boys
d girls should lose the sense of family life which home fosters. Family
e is the foundation of the welfare of a civilized community. Dickens
rote: "In love of home the love of country has its rise." Speeches
om able men in the House of Lords will be illuminating when Mr.
utler's Bill finally comes before it. He has a generous grasp of all
ese educational points.

Again, when people are discussing the new world in front of us
me will give the first place to economics, others to politics, though
is difficult to see how the world can be developed without the two
eing taken together; and we must not forget what the Bishop of
nichester has written: "Something more profound than a political
economic change is required. What is needed is a spiritual trans-
rmation in the very depths of men's hearts, through the working
the spirit and through prayer."

Opinions change. For many years there has been a controversy
the subject of tariffs. In England it was long thought impossible
impose tariffs on imports: then came a swing of the pendulum and
riffs were tried. If there are still two schools of thought at the present
me on the subject, then what will the future hold in store? Some-
ing of the same kind may be said about State control of business
d industry. This existed in earlier centuries. It is again advocated
 some and on the other hand the idea is repudiated. In one direction
ry fortunately we do find a combination of controlled and voluntary
deavour. We see this in the work of hospitals and health services.
ere, at any rate, we may praise the spirit of combination which is
und in England.

In spiritual and ecclesiastical concerns we find similar divergencies,
ough these are not debated in the House.

Some will maintain that Church and State have wholly independent
heres of influence, that it is out of place that there should be a public
cognition of faith and worship in the activities of State enterprise.
his is not the view that has been generally held in England. We
e not content to say that a man should keep his spiritual life to
mself, and that one who desires to keep the standards and the vision
 God before him is free to do this in his private devotional life. It
 our way to uphold a national recognition of God and to refuse to
ave God and His standards out of account when we come to the
ovements of public life. Such variety of views reaches the very
undations of our faith. We have only to think of the different
mphasis in the matter of faith and works as laid down by St. James

and St. Paul respectively. And some, with the gospels in their hand
put the stress upon the Incarnation of our Lord while others mainta
that His work of Atonement comes before all else. The truth is tha
both are really necessary, and that while the Incarnation of the Lor
sanctified all human life and brought Him into the world as the crow
of the human race, yet that race required His work of Atonemen
before it could be put into a position of rising to the highest of whic
it is capable in union and fellowship with Him.

In regard to all these rival views and politics the right course
probably evolved by a large and comprehensive view of the whol
it is not so much that our own view may be wrong, but that the vie
of others may also be right. It would be a great mistake if in th
contribution we are each called to make towards the establishment
the better order which it is hoped will succeed the conclusion of th
war, we merely stressed our own opinions and left those of others ou
of account; certainly in this case we are wise to be humble and no
to be too cocksure that our own attitude is the one which ought t
prevail over all.

Such is the outlook of the man of judgment, and even if he is no
greeted with the popularity which is given to one who looks straigh
towards a goal of his own making and wins the plaudits of others o
his way to it, he will be a steadying influence upon public opinio
and will carry weight even when he is not winning praise.

One must prevent any confusion arising between judgment an
intuition which by some people is supposed to be a specially feminin
quality. One who is to judge wisely will not rely upon opinions reache
without clear arguments behind them. Intuition may often be wron
and sometimes it characterizes persons who speak before they thinl
Such people will not care to hear what can be said against the conclusio
which at one spring they have reached. Hitler's 'intuition' is a by-wor
'Reflect before you decide' is a wiser motto. The man of judgment
whether he has or has not a place in the House of Lords, must reach
broad and considered view of the various elements which go to mak
up the whole. He will have reasons for what he thinks and says.
is, of course, all the better if he is the possessor of insight. But hi
insight is based upon a large acquaintance with men and things an
a careful observation and remembrance of what he has learnt, as wit
open eyes he steps through the world.

CHAPTER XXXIII

Speeches

IS DIFFICULT for bishops to take their part in the House of Lords. ɔishop, with his many diocesan engagements, many of them planned g beforehand, does not find it easy to be in London at the time fixed a debate, especially when the date is liable to alteration at the last ɔment. The result of this is that the responsibility of House of rds discussions falls heavily on the Archbishop of Canterbury l on bishops living near London, though there are occasions for ɔcial subjects when bishops gather in the House in large numbers. appened to be in the House when a debate arose on the subject of ding speeches, which proved to be an interesting topic; in my n mind it is closely related to the subject of sermons and preachers. ough the debate took place on a Derby Day there was a remarkable endance and, if I remember correctly, many important persons ve some account of their experiences; one of them, for example, scribing Mr. Gladstone (whom I only once heard in Parliament) lding unseen a very small paper in the palm of his hand that it ght be ready when he came to his peroration. It was a discussion great interest, and to the remark of one speaker who said that the ɔuse of Lords provided an icy audience, enough to quell anyone who dressed it, a rejoinder should be made that the House of Lords lges the speakers by what they have to say. It is not more cold to ɲew speaker, if he has something useful to add to the debate, than one whom it has often heard speaking before; there are, of course, tain speakers who tend to empty the House. It would not be ɔper to mention any names, but there have been certain long-winded ɛakers who, when they rose from their seats, gave the signal for going tea.

Written speeches were condemned on various accounts, and one ɯo, as an important officer of the House, had heard many debates, ld me afterwards that his experience had shown that short speeches ɛ the more effective. There is more hurry to-day and the House of ɔrds does not usually sit for many hours on one day. I ventured to ggest that it is the typewriter which is largely responsible for the ɯding of long written speeches.

It was said of Archbishop Tait that no public question was ɲsidered to have been adequately discussed until the Archbishop d expressed his opinion on the subject, often, of course, speaking

in the House of Lords. Bishop Magee was an eloquent speaker
those days, as was also Bishop Wilberforce. For those were days
which the strictly Ecclesiastical Assemblies offered less scope for m
of mark. Archbishop Benson was not as successful in the House
Lords as his predecessor; he was never quite at home there, a
however good and telling his points might be, his manner was again
him, and he had not the art of concluding with some fine statement
his views to make a climax to his speech. Archbishop Davids
carried great weight and authority; but his speeches were almc
too painstaking. He had thought out all that was to be said for
against the view he was expounding, and however good his speech
were, sometimes he gave a feeling of prolixity. Archbishop Lo
Lang is excellent; both the lucidity of what he has to say and h
eloquence in putting it forward have made him one of the very be
speakers in the whole House. The present Archbishop of York
well known as a careful expounder of any subject and wins attentio
This was not the case with Bishop Gore, for he never knew when
stop. His reiteration and his very earnestness tended to be borin
An old-fashioned speaker to whom it was for me always a delight
listen was Lord Curzon. He used long sentences, but everything alwa
ended quite straight and perfect, and I remember once when I me
tioned to him the pleasure it was to hear him for this very reason, l
seemed quite flattered, as if he were a beginner in the art. Lo
Crewe has a hesitating manner, as he pauses for exactly the rig
word, but, as would be expected, his choice of language and expressic
is perfect. In Lord Simon the House has a very notable speake
all that he says is exceedingly lucid and he is one of those men wl
puts what he has to say concisely but fully and in a way that mak
one wish to agree with him.

It was a remarkable thing to hear Lord Birkenhead explaining
subject. His manner was not suited to the House of Lords, as l
showed little respect for its formalities and dignity. I am alwa
rather sorry to have heard him speak after his illness: for then he w
a broken man, the inspiration had gone. I remember that in speakir
in a country constituency, for once his speech missed the mark. Tl
candidate for a seat in the House of Commons had arranged for
succession of speakers to follow one another in the main towns of tl
constituency. When a new speaker arrived his predecessor mov
on to the next place. When F. E. was speaking the clock struck ni
and, referring to the existing Government, he said: "The very clo
on the Town Hall agrees with you and me. Listen! It is sayin
'Ring out the old, ring in the new'." This was received with remarkab
applause. The next evening, when speaking in another town, he ma

actly the same remark when a clock again struck nine. But there
as no applause. He learnt afterwards that the previous speaker,
ptivated by F. E.'s success the night before, had used the quotation:
'ing out the old, ring in the new', as the clock had struck eight.

Lord Buckmaster possessed the gifts of a true orator, but it appeared
me that, possibly owing to ill-health, he deteriorated at the end of
s career. I remember him once over the tea-table taking part in
discussion about a cathedral servant whose business it was to carry
oney collected during the services into the vestry. The man con-
antly took something from these collections for himself. He was
tired, I think with a pension, by the Cathedral authorities who,
wever, took no proceedings against him. It was paradoxically
aintained by some of the lawyers at the table that the man had not
en guilty of theft because during his carrying the money to the
estry it belonged to nobody. The donors of the coins had parted
ith them, and the charities for which the money had been collected
ad not yet received them. Who had the right to prosecute? It
as the Almighty who had been robbed!

During the twenty-five years that I sat in the House of Lords I
bserved the weight that was carried by the Judicial Members of
ıe House—men like Lord Buckmaster, Lord Sumner, Lord Atkin,
ord Haldane, and others. It was strange that so many of them
poke inaudibly, notably Lord Haldane, but certainly their presence
nriched the House.

It may be said in passing that the same style of speech does not
uit every congregation or every assembly. A speaker or a preacher
ıust identify himself with his hearers, and grasp their capacity and
heir outlook and remember that some minds are more agile than
thers. This has led to the dictum that at a public meeting, when the
ptake of people is so different, an old joke is much more telling than a
ew one, unless the way has been very carefully prepared for the latter.

There is still great power in the pulpit for a preacher who has
omething to interest and to help his congregation. It is doubtful
f all the clergy are quick to realize whether they are gripping those
vho are listening: and they certainly will not do so if their sermons
onsist of a topical exposition of current events when it would be
uite easy for their hearers, even in a cheap magazine, to secure a
etter review of the same subject People desire in a sermon to hear
omething about God; something to help them in their character and
onduct; and to remind them of Him of whom it was said: 'Never
ıan spake like this man.' The sermons which carry in them a gospel
nessage, put in beautiful or arresting language, are the sermons which
ell.

Probably it is best for every speaker to think out for himself the style of preparation which helps him most. Some preachers find that they preach best if they have written out, perhaps two or three times over, the sermon they mean to deliver, and then learn it by heart and produce it without any reference to notes. For both preachers and speakers, the manner and gesture are important. The gestures of Mr. Lloyd George have always been graphic and telling and appropriate to what he is saying, really illustrating it. Lord Rosebery had a magnificent manner of speaking, and I have heard him give an after-dinner speech in such an impressive and compelling style that one was almost disappointed when one came to read it in the morning. I have always understood that Disraeli was a wonderful actor and that he could come into the House with an air of dejection, as if his case was hopeless, and then startle everybody by the success with which he would defend it; then he would leave with the appearance of quite a different man.

A speaker must not be selfish. If he starts early he must remember those who are going to follow. This sort of mistake is sometimes made at clerical meetings. A clergyman will read a paper, very likely an excellent paper, but it is supposed to be followed by a discussion, and if the reader of the paper has said everything possible upon the topic the discussion degenerates into a feeble expression of thanks for what his audience has heard from him.

After-dinner speaking is a special art. It must be quick and sympathetic, and there is no reason that every such speech should begin with an amusing anecdote: if it must be told, it is well now and then to let it be embodied later in the speech. But I have seen the invitation to speak after dinner really abused when a man, reading aloud a speech already in writing, goes on with it page after page until the audience is quite weary and the members of it forget that he is, however important, one of the guests like themselves. I have sometimes thought that it might occasionally be possible to deal with such a speaker by saying on the invitation card that dinner will be served at a certain hour and that half an hour before dinner XYZ will give an address on such and such a subject. Many would come to the lecture if the speaker was a well-known man and his subject vitally concerned the occasion of the dinner. Neither after dinner, nor indeed at any other time, must a speech become a lecture.

No rules can be given for composing or delivering sermons or speeches. Someone has said that if your mind is full of a subject the words will come at the time, that it is only necessary to think and think again of the various aspects of it which you desire to elucidate and you need not attempt to rehearse in your own mind how you are oing to express yourself. Lord Hastings is a very effective exponent of this style. This may be true of people of some temperaments, but phrases will not come to everyone, and even if this is a man's goal and ambition, it would need much practice before it is likely to become successful.

We learn to speak by speaking.

The saddest occasion on which I found myself speaking in the House of Lords was after the assassination of Sir Henry Wilson. Sir Henry was invited to unveil a War Memorial at Liverpool Street station to the men who fell in the 1914-18 War.

I was asked to dedicate the Memorial. Lord Claud Hamilton, Chairman of the Line, got out of a sick bed in order to take his part in the ceremony. When it was over, I went to chat with him in his room, and perhaps I was there for an hour. Leaving him, I went to the House of Lords and heard the shocking news of the assassination of Sir Henry by two Sinn Feiners on his way back from the railway station. The House of Lords was rather bewildered as to the right thing to do on such a sudden occasion. Appropriate speeches were made and to these I ventured to add my voice. The House was deeply moved—indeed I heard that Lord Rosebery said he had heard that it had never been touched so much on any other occasion—not indeed by any eloquence of mine, but by a simple recital of facts. I venture to append what I then said:

"My Lords, it is always a very solemn thing to be with a man and then to hear in a few hours that he has been cut off. Such, however, is my sad fate to-day. Sir Henry Wilson and I were at Liverpool Street Station to-day, not four hours ago, each taking his own part in the unveiling of the beautiful monument there erected to the soldiers of the Great Eastern Railway who fell in the war. He stood here—every inch a man and every inch a soldier, and he had in front of him many, many men and women whose hearts were touched to tears as he spoke to them. Somehow, it now seems appropriate that his last words should have been words of comfort to those who were mourning their lost ones as we now mourn for him. He spoke very beautifully and he spoke very briefly. Then he heard the last words about the peace of God which passeth all understanding, and that peace is now his. Then he heard the Last Post. We are glad to know that that was immediately followed by the Réveillé, and that, too, he has now heard. His speech consisted almost entirely of two quotations, one from an English poet and one from a Latin poet, Horace.

"Somehow, in the last few hours, since I heard of his tragic death and since he and I were speaking together—before we bade each other farewell—of the great soldier Lord Roberts, who was a common

friend of us both—since that time I have found running in my hea
not the words of Rudyard Kipling, nor the words of Horace, but
thought of the wonderful description given in Virgil's masterpiece
those who are entitled to enter upon the Elysian Fields. Your Lor
ships will remember that one class of those happy mortals consists
those '*Qui que sui memores alios fecere merendo*—who have built the
own memorial by the services they have rendered. Such was he an
such is he."

CHAPTER XXIV

The Lighter Side

IN WRITING THESE recollections it has been my wish, if I could, t
prevent them being too heavy. My memories for the most consist
short sketches, not elaborated essays. I have had no desire to publis
a solemn volume containing no lighter matter which may raise a smil
Men holding a public office often find that their work has its humorou
episodes, and when they come across them 'it cheers the day'.
frequently happens that in the lives of us all laughter and sadnes
are near to one another, and the same incident, viewed from differen
angles, will sometimes call out the one, sometimes the other. Let m
illustrate what is in my mind by mentioning a dear old couple wh
were very eager to be confirmed and to receive the Holy Communior
but they were too old and infirm to reach any distant confirmatio
centre. When their parish priest wrote to me about them, I tol
him I was constantly motoring in all directions, and one day, whe
I was in his neighbhourhood, I would call at their cottage and confirr
them. He was delighted, but when he brought the news to them, h
found that they were by no means pleased: they changed their mind
and no longer wished to be confirmed. He did not understand wha
could have happened. But in the end he learnt that they felt that i
I came on purpose to their cottage I should ask for a very large fee
When, however, they heard that they need pay nothing, thei
enthusiasm returned, and I confirmed them. Was this more touchin
or more amusing?

Personally, I am always against any collection taking place in
church after a confirmation. It is readily open to misconception
and it may be supposed that the bishop or the clergy presentin

ndidates are receiving some gratuity. It does not really help the
atter if the bag or plate is not handed to the candidates themselves.
A volume of funny stories, some fresh, some stale, makes heavy
ading; no one can enjoy a string of them. It is like trying to master
book of riddles. But when the stories relate to scenes from real
ppenings they are lit up through the sympathy which attaches to
man life and human nature. The only thing is that such tales grow
th the telling of them when they are recounted in isolation, especially
the case of sketches which have not fallen within one's own experi-
ce. For instance, I did not personally hear the remark of a good
oman belonging to one of the Free Churches who, when she was
noyed at some treatment she had received from her fellows,
claimed: "If this sort of thing goes on, I shall give up religion and
in the Church of England." Nor did I see the exploit of a clerical
clist anxious for reprisals. The widow lady of the village lived in
e large house which had a small park facing its big windows. It
as divided by a sunk road from the next estate. As one looked from
e windows across the road, the two properties appeared to be one.
e gave a garden party, but she had had some difference with her
ergyman and did not invite him to it. He made his protest by
ending the afternoon bicycling to and fro along the road which was
t deep enough to hide him mounted on his cycle.

How miserable is the manner in which squires and clergy so often
me to grief. I can think of a parish where there were two rival
uires and one made a protest to the clergyman because the collecting
g had been handed first to the other. But it is indeed a happy
ing before God and men when the Parsonage and the Hall join
nds and pull together without any envy or self-importance or
uchiness.

It was very unfortunate that an angry conversation took place
tween a vicar and his curate in the vestry after service one Sunday.
he organ was playing very loudly so that they had to raise their
ices to carry on their altercation, but the music that was being
ayed had a silent bar before the last. The curate had lifted up his
ice to make an opprobrious remark to the vicar: in the sudden
lence it was heard all over the church and the next day the vicar
ld me all about it, though he did not repeat what the curate had
id. I suppose that, as we used to say of Æsop's Fables, this story
aches us that it is a mistake as well as an irreverence to indulge in
dispute in church.

Years ago a man whom I scarcely knew came up to me on the
latform at Ipswich just before my train was starting, and he said:
I saw our parson a few days ago and I told him just what you think

of him." I trembled, for I had no idea how he would have interpre
any thoughts I had. This gentleman went on to remark that it v
time that I moved the man in question away from the parish. Wl
I inquired what kind of a welcome he would be likely to get from
new parishioners he replied: "We have had him for ten years and
think it is time that somebody else had a turn."

It is difficult to deal with local friction without making matt
worse, or to dispose of an undesirable incumbent; for there is no cl
and satisfactory tabulation of the enactments concerning the vari
items which come up. They must be mastered by study and exp
ence. It is impossible to act as if there was a welcome waiting for s
a man somewhere else, even so much welcome as was contained in
estimate of a new parson: "He won't do no harm to no one, he won'
an old villager was heard to say of his new parson. The parishion
now have a greater say in the choice of a new clergyman, and they
almost certain to communicate with the parish he proposes to le
and to hear a full account of it all if he has an unsatisfactory reputati

All these parochial disputes are very pitiful, but sometimes fr
their unexpected developments would make one smile if the wh
thing were not so sad. I remember a clergyman telling me abou
parishioner with whom he was unpopular, who came to see him, a
while they were shaking hands the visitor aimed the contents o
syphon of soda-water at his face and his aim was so good that
poor clergyman was drenched. This must have involved mi
premeditation and practice.

Questions relating to marriage raise many searchings of heart
bishops, and are responsible for some awkward situations.
sometimes marriages disclose a lighter and unromantic side. A bri
groom married in harvest-time and was very busy over it. So he s
to the bride: "I am too much occupied to have a honeymoon; but h
is some money for you, and please go and take a honeymoon
yourself."

A widow made no secret of it that her motive for getting marri
again was to make a 'ome for Violet (her little girl); she went on
explain: "There was a time when I sez to meself, ' 'oo'l I 'ave?' t
now it's ' 'oo'l 'ave me?' " A widower bridegroom meant no d
courtesy when he said that he merely wanted to find the kettle rea
when he got home at night. It was, I think, a touching complime
when a poor woman who had just lost her husband said of hi
"He was more like a friend than a husband."

Bishops receive many anonymous letters. I remember one
the beautiful handwriting of a child, who said: "Do you think it rig
that our clergyman should say of us children that we are little cl

vils? I don't"; and then the signature appended was: "One of the le clay devils." Another letter showed a dreadful misapprehension the meaning of Prayer when it stated: "My neighbour has done me great injury; your prayers count for more than mine; kindly pray at a misfortune may overtake her."

We ourselves must be careful to choose our prayer well. A prominent clergyman was rebuking a well-educated man who was given drink. The latter took it well, but before they parted the clergyman ayed the collect which asks God by His strength and protection to ry us through all temptations; the prayer opens by saying that "by son of the frailty of our nature we cannot always stand upright". is was regarded by the offender as taking a mean advantage and s not forgiven.

These things are not pointless anecdotes, but they illustrate some the features of life among all classes with which the clergy, and hind them the bishop, have to deal. But one likes to remember at however much villagers appear to be prone to quarrel, they will, a case of need, be altogether unselfish and kindhearted if some less or misfortune overtakes a neighbour.

I decided to spend my summer holiday at Yarmouth during the t war. I went to see the house offered to me a month beforehand I was accompanied by an old pupil of mine who was at that time a prominent position in the Expeditionary Force. We carried our . with us in a bag and took it on the beach near a little barbed wire ce that ran along in front of the sea. When we had finished we nt up on to the parade and were arrested by a sergeant. He must ve thought that I looked a suspicious character, carrying my black g, wearing a bishop's hat with an alpaca coat, for it was a hot day. haded myself with a white foreign umbrella with a green lining. were requested to walk to the headquarters close by. My companion was indignant. I was chiefly anxious not to lose the train ck to Norwich. We were put to wait in a small room while the geant made his report to the Territorial Captain then in command. ter a few minutes we were admitted to his presence. My friend was uniform and duly showed his papers. I could only show the tea- ps, etc., in my bag, and mention who I was. In a few moments we re discharged and, to show there was no ill will, I asked the Captain tell me the shortest way to the station. My companion was upset the incident and said he pitied the Sergeant who had arrested us, en he thought what was in store for him in the Sergeants' mess that ht.

It was rather a curious thing that some years afterwards when a lunch I mentioned to two or three young men what had happened,

one of those present good-humouredly remarked: "I have heard th
story of yours before, and I heard it from the Territorial Captain
A few years went by and I was told in Norwich that Sergeant —
would like to see me. When I went into the room I found that he w
the sergeant who had arrested me, and he spoke very nicely and sa
that he hoped that I bore him no ill will. We parted excellent frien

CHAPTER XXXV

Marriage and Divorce

I HAVE UNFORTUNATELY differed from many of the other bishops
certain aspects of the perplexing subject of divorce. My opinio
and my remarks cannot pretend to be exhaustive or to cover all t
historical, social, and doctrinal aspects of a difficult matter. Perha
I shall be rather stating some of the questions involved than attempti
to solve them. It may be that my true motto is: 'Prevention is bett
than cure.' The whole subject has in recent years been fully examin
in the assemblies of the Church, in parliamentary debates and
private discussions. The last war increased the number of unhap
marriages. Young men and women turned to marriage in the exci
ment of the time, when a young woman would look upon a soldier
a hero, without any thought of the responsibilities involved in marryi
him. The equalization of the sexes has facilitated what are call
'hotel divorces', often involving perjury.

Marriage is the one point in which the Church alters the ci
status of the parties and, this being so, there may arise conflicts
opinion between Church law and civil law, and any such discrepan
may lead to trouble. It has been suggested that any possible div
gence might be removed by a scheme of civil marriage all roun
but this would not really save the situation because sooner or lat
the question of admissibility to the Holy Communion would aris
this point is complicated by the fact that the Prayer Book, includi
the rubrics about the open and notorious evil liver, is a part of the l
of the land—being attached to an Act of Parliament.

It may be noted that it is difficult for the Church of Engla
to ignore the rest of Christendom, and when we speak of the Chur
of England, we must remember that facilities are provided now

e Law for Free Church Ministers solemnizing a marriage. The
eek Church has its own views and ways. So has the Church of
ome which, while rejecting all divorce can, by other means, find a way
und. Among us, good churchmen have held divergent opinions.
chbishop Davidson was satisfied with the law, allowing divorce in
rtain cases, as it stood in his day. The saintly Bishop King of
ncoln did not condemn all divorce, but the Matrimonial Causes Act
1937 has put a new complexion upon the position, extending widely,
it does, the grounds for divorce.

In the Church of England great emphasis has lately been laid upon
e apparent discrepancy between the Gospel of St. Matthew on one
le, and the Gospels of St. Luke and St. Mark on the other. The
ords of St. Matthew permit divorce in certain circumstances. The
her two Gospels admit of no exception to the abiding permanence of
arriage. It has been widely maintained that the words of our Lord
St. Mark and St. Luke are authoritative and that St. Matthew, for
natever cause, has departed from them. This is, of course, a
ngerous attitude to adopt; it is too late to change the habits and
aditions of the people by an appeal to historical criticism of the
xt of Holy Scripture. What we desire to know is the mind of the
ord; it is this that helps us much more than would a shorthand
port of His words. We want to learn what was felt to be the meaning
what He said. We cannot be certain that He would always say
e same thing on one subject, if any reason for amplification or
ntraction arose; nor was it Our Lord's way to legislate on particular
ints. He gives the principles of a new life. The last words of St.
atthew's Gospel have been regarded as the charter of foreign missions,
it these words as they stand are certainly not found in St. Mark or
. Luke, yet those who would repudiate the form of St. Matthew's
ords on the subject of divorce do not attack His words on foreign
issions in the same manner.

We must be very careful not to lower the moral standard nor to
lopt an easy-going way of saying that there is no reason in this,
in other matters, to draw a distinction between the Christian
ind and the unchristian level. Yet we cannot act in ordinary life
ith strict rigidity. Our practice is to take large views and to find
place for charity and considerateness: for example, it would seem
npossible—to some people—that a woman who can be clearly recognized
s the innocent party in a divorce suit, and has been driven to divorce
brutal husband, should be excluded from the Holy Communion
nless some disciplinary action has first been taken by the Church.
an she reasonably be considered an open and notorious evil liver?
Ve may have our own views, and hold them strongly; but where others

can with any show of reason differ from us, we can scarcely condemn
them outright. In spite of the Mothers' Union, we can see that the
sanctity of marriage is not the same as its indissolubility. Devout
upholders of its sanctity find some place for divorce. It is not absurd
for them to suggest that St. Matthew's exception may admit of the
possibility of the existence of other exceptions which also wreck the
whole idea of a true union.

We have to do all that we can to prevent undesirable marriages
and to teach the newly married not to let the first bloom of married
love fade away. Growing boys and girls should hear these things
explained plainly and simply: many of them suffer from a kind of
conspiracy of silence. If they do not hear the subject being spoken
of reverently and tenderly, they may grow up in deplorable ignorance
that can spoil a happy marriage association; if they do not learn the
right view from the right people they may learn a very wrong view
from the wrong people.

I would like to say that it is kind to give a hint to the newly married
to take pains—for all things worth having need thought and care—
not to let their married life deteriorate. In the last war and this
war-work has been the enemy of affectionate home life. Some years
ago I wrote a little book on marriage in which occur these words that
are true: "All the fine courtesies of married life and the brightness of
its devotion, the little attentions, which once were the pretty tokens
of affection, gradually disappear if each exacts more than he or she
offers. A man may become so immersed in his business, a woman in
her duties or amusements, that, when they meet, it is rather for dispute
and fault-finding or dreary absent-minded dullness, than for love and
peace together . . ."

We cannot expect that those who are married can give all their
time and all their thought to one another. But there are two things
they can do: first of all they can see to it that they do not let their
children engross all their affections and thus draw them apart from
one another. Secondly, they can make sure that, however busy they
are and however full the day must be with other calls and other
claims, they seize every chance when they do meet to make much of
one another, and again and again to show to each other that he or she
still stands first. The secret of a happy home is found by those who
always keep near to one another in Christ. Their marriage is by Him
transfigured into the *Holy Matrimony* of the Prayer Book.

However eager we may be to prevent unfortunate marriages, we
often appear too late upon the scene, and in war time even more
than at other times, there is a general excitement abroad which
induces young people to marry before they know one another so

timately as to become friends for life as well as husbands and wives.
am afraid we commonly make the mistake of hesitating to speak
early and affectionately of marriage and family life to children
d young people as soon as they can understand something of what
being said to them. I am not forgetting the delicate and strong
otection there is to be found in innocence; we have to be careful
speak in such a way as not to spoil its bloom. The duty primarily
sts upon fathers and mothers and the clergy, not so much the duty
speaking themselves as the responsibility for seeing that the young
e wisely taught. Some people have felt a reluctance against speaking
their own children; in some cases the affinity between them makes
obstacle, though probably, in many cases, a mother can speak
ith a great and attractive sympathy to her boys. The right person
speak must be thoughtfully chosen; for example a wise doctor
n be called in, if he is a good fellow and a tactful Christian. It is
kely enough that children will ask questions on such a subject at a
ery early date, and it is a mistake to put them off with evasive
plies, or to tell them such silly things as that the doctor has brought
new brother or sister in his bag. They can be taught through the
ets they keep, or the flowers they grow in their own little gardens, or
other ways, directed by science, or a mother's understanding.

CHAPTER XXXVI

The Prayer Book

NOTHER IMPORTANT ISSUE in which I found myself differing from
early all my episcopal colleagues was the revision of the Prayer Book
1927 and the following year. But I have no desire to write a detailed
eview of old controversies, and I would sooner think of the friends
gained at the time than of friends whom I am afraid I lost. I should
ever have reached the same intimacy with the former if we had not
ome close together in the debates. Among them I may mention
ord Caldecote, Bishop Knox, Mr. Guy Johnson, 'Jix' (as the late
ord Brentford was affectionately called by his friends), Lord Cushen-
en, Lord Lincolnshire, Lord Carson, Lord William Cecil, Bishop of
xeter. What a joy it was to welcome the Bishop as 'my twin', when he
elegraphed from abroad to put himself by my side. They and I were

very ready that a Prayer Book two hundred and fifty years old shou
be brought up to date, to meet some modern needs which had natural
grown up since 1662. This was the course recommended in 1906 I
the Royal Commission on Ecclesiastical Discipline.

Speaking for myself, I opposed the book which was finally reject
in 1927 and again on its reappearance with slight amendments
1928 for the following reasons, and more recently I have declare
myself against any proposals that have tended in the same directio
I made a note of these reasons after the conclusion, so far as it was
conclusion, of the discussions. I objected to the new Prayer Bo
because:

(1) In my humble opinion it was not in the line of *English* devotio

(2) Though not intended to do so, in the judgment of many, a
in my own, it did alter the doctrine of the present Book.

It was said to be only a question of emphasis; but, after all, emphas
is an integral part of our apprehension of and approach to God. 'W
see through a glass darkly.'

(3) I doubted whether the bishops could successfully make go
their promise to enforce its regulations.

(4) I drew a great distinction between the unauthorized practi
of new methods of worship and any official authorization of them.

(5) A book, intended to meet new needs, resuscitated ways
devotion which Englishmen had discarded.

(6) It would have been a disaster to change the present Bo
beyond recall, and later to have found that the new line wou
inevitably once more be overstepped; the result being that nothi
would have been gained and much lost.

(7) The Church Assembly does not as yet adequately represe
the mind of the Church of England.

This is specially true of the devout worshippers in parish churche
I do not wish to amplify these points now, and I am not now sayir
anything about the workmanship of the Book which has been co
demned as faulty by careful and scholarly criticism. At the tim
public meetings were held, articles and pamphlets published. Whe
I had stepped aside from the meetings of the whole body of bisho
who were considering the matter I wrote in the papers to explain m
opposition.

The whole controversy had a curious effect upon my position a
a bishop of the Church of England: I did not bear the label of a stror
Evangelical leader before I came to be identified with many Eva
gelicals, with whom I then worked; I preferred to follow the lead
my great master, Bishop Westcott of Durham, who, I think, describe
himself as a historic churchman. It was as an Englishman that

as against sanction being given to the new Book; but many of those who joined in opposing it were out-and-out Evangelicals. In public estimation and general reputation it is usual for a man to be classed among those with whom he is working. I have always, however, maintained my own independence of judgment and outlook. It may be noted that some extreme Anglo-Catholics joined in condemning the Book, as also did many Free churchmen who regard the Prayer Book—as it stands—as one of the pillars of our national recognition of God. We were a mixed, motley, and miscellaneous crowd, and I even became a hero to some members of the Anglo-Catholic section as we united on this issue with one another, though our motives were divergent.

I remember the occasion when I announced to the bishops—sitting round the great table at Lambeth—that I proposed to withdraw from their deliberations, and that I should leave no step, open to a Christian and a gentleman, untried, in my effort to oppose their decision. They listened kindly and patiently but obviously with pity for me in my futile folly. When in the end the new Prayer Book was rejected, I felt that I was regarded as one of the guilty culprits in the result, and that the bishops' pity was now changed into indignation. There are few survivors among those who took part in the discussions, but I have always felt that the shadow of the old censure has rested upon me. I had already told Archbishop Davidson what I was proposing to do and I showed him the letter I intended to offer to *The Times*. He remarked that if I did intend to write to *The Times* he could find no fault with my letter. I had proposed to send the letter directly after I had dissociated myself from the bishops, but he asked me to wait, lest I should create an impression that the bishops were more divided than they were. I am always glad that I assented. I had no wish to steal a march on him. Before the bishops' proposals were published he had a Press Conference, as we should now term it; and to begin with, the Press supported him; but as the months went by people began to think. They saw, too, that the Archbishop and I were able to differ on a public matter without bitterness.

I doubt whether, at the time, before the final judgment of Parliament was given, the deep religious feeling of Englishmen was apprehended. Englishmen are reluctant to express their intimate spiritual convictions. They do not in our generation welcome religious controversy which three hundred years ago constantly appealed to their predecessors. Nevertheless many of them did eagerly set themselves against the proposed changes in the Prayer Book. Dr. D'Arcy, the Archbishop of Armagh and Primate of Ireland at the time, when he was to speak upon the relation between Church and State, used words

of great importance with reference to the significance of the inter
roused by the Prayer Book discussions.

"We are often told that, in the modern world, the majority
men and women are indifferent in the matter of religion. That ficti
is now exploded. No question in recent times has so deeply stirr
the hearts and minds of the people of Great Britain as did the Pray
Book question. How eagerly were the debates read and the decisio
regarded by the whole nation! The Press in foreign countries w
filled with expressions of astonishment that a religious issue shou
so engross the attention of modern people. Now that is a tremendo
fact, infinitely more important than any of the special questio
debated at the time. I confess to a real amazement that this aspe
of the subject has not received more attention. It means that,
spite of all appearances to the contrary, the people of Great Brita
are profoundly interested in religion."

It certainly was a notable event that a Book promoted by the tw
Archbishops and all the English bishops, with, I think, the excepti
of four, and having the support of *The Times* newspaper and of t
Prime Minister of the day and the advocacy of Lord Quickswood
great churchman whose goodness and considerateness have w
widespread affection and made him a powerful leader, should ha
been rejected twice over by Parliament, when a few changes in wh
were considered vital matters might have turned the scale.

The conflict of opinion apparently was sharp and severe; elsewhe
however, I have said enough about the relation between Church a
State. Usually Englishmen, even after forcible disagreements, wh
a contest is over, good-humouredly are willing to remove any acrimo
which may have been aroused and to respect and work with o
another again. However serious the difference of principles betwe
them may have been, the assertion of it does not make personal a
lasting enemies between members of the two sides. But this spi
of mutual forbearances and 'give and take' has scarcely been observa
in this particular matter. Perhaps this has been the case because t
contest related to things which are always with us, and therefo
unlike some strictly political and limited issue, it did not come to
end and settle down when the matter in question seemed to be ov
Spiritual and religious divergences go very deep.

I think this short sketch is adequate for my purpose, and I ha
written it because I did not consider that it would be right for me,
looking back upon my ecclesiastical memories, to be silent upon
important subject in regard to which I was pushed into a more or l
prominent situation. My action, too, has affected my career.

THE BISHOP OF NORWICH AND MRS. POLLOCK, 1935

CHAPTER XXXVII

Edith Cavell

SOME WAYS I was rather closely associated with the final stages
the beautiful career of Edith Cavell. After she had been killed by
: Germans I went to see her aged mother as soon as possible, and
and her in the tiny home which Edith helped to maintain in Norwich.
e was the widow of a fine old clergyman, Rector of Swardeston,
ar Norwich, and Edith had a large share of her father's ability and
aracter. It will be remembered that the shooting of Edith Cavell
ead a sense of horror through the world, and there was held a special
rvice in St. Paul's after the sad event. It is likely that her death
ought home to the Americans what the war meant.

On the first day I visited her, Mrs. Cavell was bewildered; her
tle room was strewn with letters and telegrams. She thought me
ite clever when I suggested that it would be quite enough to send
ne printed expression of her gratitude, instead of trying to answer
ery one separately. It was difficult for her at her advanced age to
spond to suggestions made to her from various quarters. I remember
elegram from Australia saying: *We have collected some thousands of
unds to commemorate your brave daughter. Please telegraph how you
uld wish it spent.* It was one of the ironies of such a situation that
ose who wrote to Mrs. Cavell had not imagined that Edith had
atributed to the maintenance of her mother in her little house, and
at in consequence Mrs. Cavell was left in a very poor financial
sition. Later, we were able, through the Civil List, to secure a
nsion for her remaining years.

Mrs. Cavell, in all her grief and distress, fully recognized that her
ughter had exceeded the right course in passing recovered prisoners
rough the hospital, thus enabling them to find safety outside the
untry. She spoke of Edith as if she were still a child, remarking:
Edith did what she shouldn't."

I still vividly recall the lovely spring evening in 1919 with the
acs in bloom, when after the long journey from abroad and through
ndon, her body was laid to rest near the Cathedral in Norwich. The
ace where it was interred then bore the name of Life's Green (now
ich of this lawn is occupied by the War Memorial Chapel subsequently
ded to the Cathedral).

Her example of Christian patriotism is briefly told in a record at
e grave. It is remarkable that so many people visit it; there is

F

nothing splendid about it; but many of those who come must l
upon it as a pilgrimage to her honour, and a tribute to the devot
and self-sacrifice of womanhood at its best. The simple and pregn
phrases of this record repeat her final utterances, beautiful and Chr
like: "Patriotism is not enough, I must have no hatred towards anyon

The name Life's Green is a token of her life. She said at the e
that she had seen too much of death to fear it. We like to th
of her as alive, both as she lived in this world and now lives in
nearer Presence of Christ. Life is always fresh and green to th
who live unto Him. It is not a matter of age; the point is how
are spending our life. St. Paul wrote: "To me, to live is Christ." A
we are familiar with the splendid words of the prophet: "He giv
power to the faint and to them that have no might he increas
strength. Even the youths shall faint and be weary, and the you
men shall utterly fail; but they that wait upon the Lord shall ren
their strength; they shall run and not be weary, and they shall w
and not faint." What a picture of true and vigorous life which ne
leaves its springtide behind!

We often think of the debt which England owes to the charac
and capacity of those who have been reared in its clerical hom
perhaps this was truer in days gone by when the spirit of neighbo
liness was stronger and people moved about less; the wives and fami
of clergymen were more wholeheartedly devoted to the life of
parish.

In earlier days, Norfolk had a supreme example in Nelson, w
was the son of the rector of Burnham Thorpe; and now, later,
Edith Cavell, we have added a gallant woman to the list. There
many others, perhaps less outstanding, who have set their mark up
our English National life. It may be supposed that in homes l
them there is an atmosphere of goodness, and a high standard
character. Boys and girls can, at any rate, learn in such surroundi
to look out upon life with a purpose. They associate with all sorts a
conditions of life, and learn the human touch that counts for mu
they learn through these parochial contacts the immense importan
of the simple realities of life, and can check and correct theories
practical activities. The people come again and again to the parsona
for advice and help of every kind, and the children of the parsona
see this going on about them. The best among them catch the sp
of leadership and sympathy, which helps them later with their o
responsibilities. Meanwhile they share in the village life through
games, sports, and simple entertainments, which draw the peo
together in a joint effort for the happiness and well-being of
community.

We can think of summer days in the rectory grounds and turn to such occasions as are described in Goldsmith's lines:

> *When all the village train, from labour free,*
> *Led up their sports beneath the spreading tree,*
> *While many a pastime circled in the shade,*
> *The young contending as the old surveyed;*
> *And many a gambol frolicked o'er the ground,*
> *And sleights of art and feats of strength went round.*
> *And still as each repeated pleasure tired,*
> *Succeeding sports the mirthful band inspired.*

CHAPTER XXXVIII

Burial and Faculties

MUCH MORE ATTENTION than used to be the case has been paid to the artistic side of our churches and churchyards. A hundred years ago and less the squire and the parson seemed to have things very much their own way without reference to any other authority, and no one complained. Memorials were put into the church which would never now be tolerated, and many were removed and perhaps thrown away or put to chance uses. Now the law concerning faculties is better known and more closely obeyed. Apart from altogether inconsiderable and non-contentious matters of trifling importance, a faculty must be obtained in the Consistory Court where the Chancellor of the diocese sits and decides the issue. A recent measure of the Church Assembly has, with certain restrictions, deputed some of this work to the Archdeacon in minor questions. Also there has been constituted in every diocese an Advisory Committee to help the Chancellor in dealing with the artistic side of new proposals, to prevent incongruous or unseemly additions to the interiors of the church, and to protect from changes which would spoil its beauty. There is a Central Committee in London to which the Diocesan committee can resort for guidance, and its secretary, Dr. Eales, is eager to help individuals also in the matter of taste and material.

A good Advisory Committee will deal kindly with mourners and try to lead them and will not dictate to them by mere routine rules:

even when rules must be followed, sympathy can smooth their endorsment. I used to nominate the members of our own diocesan committe and always presided at the meetings.

But it is not only strictly artistic matters that the Chancelle and the Advisory Committee have to consider. They have to observ whether an adequate connection with the Church belonged to th person to be commemorated, or whether (if he or she is a member of family already possessing some memorial in it) the proposal is i agreement with the previous designs. Everyone is not as wise a Queen Victoria, who, when after Prince Albert's death had a recumber effigy made of him had one made of herself at the same time, so tha the representations should be contemporaneous and harmoniou strangely enough, when the time came, forty years later, to put hers in its place, it could nowhere be found, until an aged man who had bee engaged in the work at Frogmore when the Prince died, recalled tha the figure of the Queen had been bricked up in the wall there at th time, to be in readiness when she, too, passed away.

The Committee is an Advisory Committee; the responsibility i every case rests with the Chancellor who, however, is naturally gla to hear the views of its members on the many points that he has consider before issuing a faculty, which we may add in all cases gran a permission, and does not give an order.

Inscriptions on memorials need close attention in regard not on to sentiments and the expression of them, but also to the style lettering and material used. All this relates to churchyards as well to churches. The clergyman has no inherent authority in the matte but he can, by custom, let some usual tombstones and ordinary desig pass: of others he can say that it would be proper to seek a facult The responsibility in such a case belongs not to the clergyman but the Chancellor; and in giving or refusing his consent the latter wi in most cases, turn to the Advisory Committee for their opinio He will take each application on its own merits. He will not, by general order, exclude the use of some particular material, but in given case he will consider how far a tombstone made of it will agr with its surroundings. From the Chancellor's decision an appeal li to the Dean of Arches, the Judge of the superior court.

In such cases trouble sometimes arises from the mourners havi already placed the order for a tombstone with a particular firm monumental masons, and later in the day it seems severe to deci against what has already been begun. For the preservation of th simple beauty of our churchyards nothing would help more than th general co-operation of the firms who provide monuments. Some these make an early application to mourners to secure their custor rwarding a catalogue of conventional designs that they recommend. emeteries do not lie in the jurisdiction of the Consistory Court, and them one can see a miscellaneous and incongruous collection of monuments, often in bad taste, which would never have passed the crutiny of an Advisory Committee.

Speaking more generally of rules concerning churchyards I may observe that in regard to funerals the use of churchyards has been modified by recent burial legislation. Moreover, the interment of a body is permissible either without any service at all, or with some other hristian and orderly service conducted by a person not in Holy Orders f the Church of England.

More frequently than might be supposed, it is desired to move a body from one consecrated place of burial to another. This can be permitted by faculty, and, at any rate in the diocese of Norwich, this pecial faculty is issued, not in the consistory court, but by the bishop himself, if he considers that the reason is adequate, as, for example, order to move a body hastily buried in one place to a family grave lsewhere. I remember well a day when such a faculty granted by the ishop was very timely. An undertaker came to see me one afternoon, nd finding me at home, poured out his story with considerable agitation. Such a misfortune had never before overtaken his firm with its ong-standing reputation. (Naturally an undertaker sees these internents, like men in another trade, from his own point of view. There vas an instance of an undertaker taking a message to one of the nourners as he was leaving the churchyard and putting it into his wn phraseology he said: "Corpse's brother would be grateful if you vould wait for him for a few minutes.") This unfortunate man had uried a body in the wrong grave owing to a pardonable confusion etween two neighbouring graves recently dug. The second funeral vas to take place next day. I congratulated him on coming to the nan who could help him, and I sent to the diocesan office and had the ecessary faculty made out and, having signed it, I handed it to the ndertaker, telling him to move the body during the night and to say nothing about it. A very different man left my study from the man vho had entered it an hour before: he was now supremely happy.

In a church or churchyard great care is needed not to offend the iving representatives of those buried or commemorated in a previous eneration. After careful inquiry has been made, these representatives till seem to spring up from nowhere! We had been repairing one of ur many lovely churches, and, at the moment the churchyard was ery untidy before the work was finished and cleared up, I received a etter of strong complaint about the state of the churchyard from a nan staying at the time in one of our seaside resorts, saying that the

grave of one of his forbears was in this neglected churchyard.
explained the position and added that as he was interested in th
matter I could tell him that the repair fund was not yet closed, an
perhaps he would wish to send me a contribution. He wrote again
but only to say that he considered my letter to be most unsatisfactory

I should here say a few words about cremation. The practice o
cremation is spreading, and war-time requirements have extended it
use. No authoritative and final suggestions or recommendations as to
the disposal of the ashes, or the point or points at which appropriate
prayers, etc., can be used, have yet been adopted; it is not easy to
have uniformity of regulation to meet the special features and require
ments of each case. But we need some more or less general observances
for the habit of cremation will spread and prejudices against it are
growing weaker. With our large populations, cemeteries necessitate
an extravagant and unwholesome use of land on the outskirts of our
cities which is appropriate for building purposes. Any feeling against
cremation is probably promoted by two considerations, the charm o
our country churchyards, and the remembrance of Our Lord's burial
We like to think of those we love sleeping in the calm beauty of the
churchyard though the thought of a cemetery is less attractive.

The story of the Resurrection is bound up with the associations o
Our Lord's burial. Anyone who in Jerusalem has visited the Garden
Tomb and reverently looked at the spot, which at least must be
similar to the sepulchre where Our Lord's Body was laid—even if it
is not the actual sepulchre—may be pardoned if he prefers burial to
cremation. But, after all, this does not go to the root of the matter
the personality will survive the disintegration of the body whether by
fire or by other slower decay, and the personality will one day be
clothed upon with a form which will correspond with the glorious
change in the life after death. 'For soul is form and doth the body
make.'

'For Christ shall change the body of our humiliation that it may
be fashioned like unto His glorious body.' It will, however, be recog-
nizable. We shall know one another in the land of beauty where
things of beauty meet. We must not mislead ourselves by dwelling
on Byron's words as if all the loveliness belonged to the retrospect:

> He who hath bent him o'er the dead
> Ere the first day of death is fled,
> The first dark day of nothingness,
> The last of danger and distress,
> Before Decay's effacing fingers
> Have swept the lines where beauty lingers,

And marks the mild angelic air,
The rapture of repose that's there,
The fixed yet tender traits that streak
The languor of the placid cheek.

The personality now beautified and glorified is what matters.

CHAPTER XXXIX

Brotherhood

BROTHERHOOD IS A very popular word in the pulpit, in the Press, and public meetings. But I do not know that it is used with any precision of meaning. Brotherhood suggests some family origin. Behind a real brotherhood must stand fatherhood, and if men are to look upon one another as brothers, they need to be linked together by the bond of one father, and the Father of all is God, from whom the whole family (or every fatherhood) in heaven and earth is named (Ephesians iii, 15). The word Father is found in the Old Testament; we shall find that it is used, and in some limited sense explained, in the Book of Isaiah. But these Old Testament phrases are not as deep as the words of Our Lord; perhaps they chiefly refer to the family of Israel, and date from Abraham. When Our Lord speaks of God as Father He does not speak of God as the common Father of Himself and us: He says: 'My Father, and your Father'. God is His Father by nature. He is our Father in more than one sense as our Creator, etc., but His fullest Fatherhood towards us is found by our adoption into Christ. When Christ speaks of the Fatherhood of God He tells us much more than that God is a source of brotherhood among men: Christ speaks of God's tenderness and His fatherly loving-kindness to all.

When, then, we speak of our brotherhood with other men we must think of our common Father if our words are to touch realities. The Father originates the one family of the human race; and if God the Father is the source of this family, Christ is the link to join together all those whom He was not ashamed to call His brethren.

We may note, when Christ became incarnate, it is said that the Word became flesh, not a man—one man among many: for He took

to Himself the whole of human nature and identified Himself wi
mankind as a whole. This thought, this truth, is what appears to
on the philosophical side the meaning of the Virgin Birth. T
Virgin Birth was not just one more miracle proclaimed in the Bib
but it made the Lord's manhood to be unenclosed. He drew a tr
human nature from His mother, but He had no human father.
the case of ourselves, our individuality is limited by our doub
parentage, and the heritage we derive from it on both sides; but th
Lord's humanity was inclusive of all. Comprehending within it th
whole of the human race of which He was and is the Head, with a
its varied characteristics, He is in touch with men and women of ever
generation, of every country, language, tradition, and outlook.
this way St. Paul is able again and again to use his favourite phras
'In Christ' to express the relations which can exist between each an
all with Him. So it has come about that the results of His work ar
available for all because He is representative of the whole numbe
and the virtue of what He has done on behalf of the race avails fo
all and is available to all. The power of His human life, and th
atonement achieved by His cross and resurrection is for us all. "Le
us therefore come boldly (saying everything) unto the Throne of Grace
that we may obtain mercy and find grace to help in time of need."

I am inclined to believe that when Our Lord speaks of Himse.
as the Son of Man He is in part indicating the same truth. The us
of this title in the New Testament is suggestive. With one exceptio
it is only used by the Lord Himself in speaking of Himself: it is foun
in each of the four Gospels. Besides this St. Stephen alone once use
it, when at the time of his death he exclaimed: "Behold I see th
heavens opened and the Son of Man standing on the right hand of God.
We commonly think of the Ascended Christ as seated—after Hi
labours were accomplished—at the right hand of the Father, in equa
glory; but on this occasion St. Stephen saw Him standing up, as if to
help him and to welcome him as he laid down his life, the first martyr
for His sake.

Different views have been held of the meaning of this title 'The
Son of Man' which I have carefully examined. There are no doub
linguistic difficulties about, it and it is not easy to be quite certai
through what channels it came to the Lord's lips. Nor is it certai
of what it was significant. Some have thought that it means no
more than Man, and passages can be quoted from the Gospel an
perhaps from other sources suggesting various interpretations for it
some of them reducing the width and depth of its meaning. Anyhow
it had come to be a title of the Messiah; in this way the Lord Himsel
appears to use it at the time of His trial before the High Priest and

s associates. But it is quite possible that the title may have had
other meaning as well, and that at the end of His life on earth the
ord drew the meanings together. If He did this the fact that He
d so would not prevent our regarding the title 'The Son of Man' as
rallel to the title 'The Son of God', the one representing His relation-
ip to God, the other His relationship to the human race, for which
e has been, from the day of the Virgin Birth onwards, the centre of
nity. More than this, if Christ gathers up into Himself all men,
ing Himself the Man of Men, then being also by nature God, He
ites this united human race to God. When we speak of the Brother-
ood of Man, etc., we do well to keep His gracious figure always before
r eyes as the focus and consecration of our unity. Coming from
od, He brings humanity, as a whole, to God.

All this does not mean that all men are equal or that all races are
qual. This is one of the false implications of a free and easy and
reless use of the word Brotherhood. In every family there is some
ariety in the members of it. The children of the same parents are
ot interchangeable. So it is with whole races. Some may have,
hether locally or nationally or internationally, the gift of leadership;
thers may be better as followers than leaders; some again may have
gift for citizenship, for holding together as members of one com-
unity; to others such a position may be foreign. Anyone can notice
e distinction between East and West. We can look to the Hindus
nd see their power of contemplation, and we can contrast them with
e practical ways of the English world. We can look at the logical
culties of the French and contrast these with our English habit of
aking little of theories, if we can make a success of our actual
terprises.

Brotherhood does not mean an equality among all men. One
nd all are of equal value in God's sight, and of this we must not be
nmindful; but it does not follow that all men in consequence can be
eated as equals in their relationship to one another. We do not
xpect a dead level of unclassified uniformity. Equality of opportunity
abling everyone to reach the best of which he is capable is a very
ifferent matter. We cannot expect all beautiful birds to mate
gether promiscuously, or that they all should eat the same food.
veryone may be equally beautiful, but one cannot take the place
f another.

We like to think of a growing brotherhood among the nations of
e world at the present time, but if what has been written is true,
e shall not dare to leave out the primary claims of God, and also,
midst the varieties shown by men, we shall need generously to make
llowances for one another, and to respect national characteristics.

F*

If we are to do this successfully we shall be wise to remember what th Prime Minister has said of beginning to plan for the new world, which each and all will have his share, while we are still at war. H has also warned us against the enemy's desire to keep the war goin so long as to weary the Allies and, through impatience, to split the present brotherhood. We shall work all the better at our task if w set about it while there is something still to be done, and somethin to bind us actively together. This will prevent our adopting an doctrinaire attitude, which was one of the misfortunes at the end of th last war. Our thoughts would be wiser and keep us closer together we are bound together by common effort in the common task. W shall think more clearly and grasp more sensibly the ways and requir ments of different peoples and men if we do not lean back an contemplate the whole situation in an academic or theoretical manne

There was a charming family feeling in the little story with whic the King concluded his broadcast on Christmas Day telling us of boy who was carrying an even smaller child up a hill. Asked wheth the heavy burden was not too much for him, the boy answered "It's not a burden, it's my brother."

Administrative plans will fail if we contemplate any institutic or organization among men as if it had no past behind it, and a if we were founding a new club and were free to make appropria rules for its membership and procedure. Above everything we hav to remember that 'Over all is humanity', and over against humanit stands the Son of Man. He lifts us into the Eternal World to whic He has ascended. It is this Eternal World on which our eyes must l fixed.

CHAPTER XL

Postscript

By Mrs. Bertram Pollock

THE FIRST TIME that I met Bertram Pollock was in Norwich whe I called at the Palace by appointment to discuss with him a seri of meetings on Church matters in which I was then interested. was led up two flights of stairs by a tall and elegant footman, an shown into the small drawing-room, where tea was laid and th

Bishop sat waiting, with his feet up on the sofa (a characteristic attitude). He received me graciously and at once disarmed me by seeing that my coat and hat were wet (it had been raining) and having them sent down to be dried. He then offered me egg sandwiches specially ordered for me, remembering that I had said I had a meeting at Lowestoft that evening, and thinking that I should get no dinner. This mixture of kindness and formality, of old-world splendour and simplicity was impressive. Here was a man, I thought, untroubled by the march of time; inaccessible except by written appointment; living in an atmosphere of monastic remoteness in an inexpressibly gloomy Palace under the shadow of a great Cathedral. This was the prelude to our friendship and marriage . . .

His first years at Norwich were lonely ones: a bachelor in an exalted position; the cynosure of all eyes; with none to whom he could turn for advice; and with grown men under his administration, not boys with open minds to teach. (How often has he lamented on the decline of human nature as it grows to maturity. Disillusionment takes the place of wonder, and often depravity or greed supplant the first vision of youth.)

Not many of the outside world were admitted to the intimate friendship of B. P. The rather aloof manner he assumed sometimes in public was a form of self-defence, but those who got beneath the surface soon found a sensitive nature that could at once make a friend of a fellow-creature, of any class or generation. His ready wit and sense of fun; the swift passage of his mind from the sublime to the ridiculous and back, made him a delightful companion, as did also his deep knowledge of human nature and of the hidden things of God.

B. P. had a singular gift for friendship, and, by his sympathy and power to put himself alongside his companion, would soon make the beginnings of a life-long friendship, maintained over long distances of time and place by correspondence. Sometimes he would meet someone in the street and pick up where he had left off years before.

Perhaps his greatest friend was his elder doctor brother, who died some thirty years ago. Had this brother lived, he would undoubtedly have been one of the leading gynæcologists of his generation These two were like David and Jonathan. His eldest brother, Ernest (who became the Master of the Rolls and took the title of Hanworth), looked after B. P. as a little boy in a grandfatherly manner (Lizzie, his nurse, called him mockingly 'Grandfather'), and in later years he told me he always felt as if he were a little boy when with Ernest. They had a deep attachment to each other, and admired the other's very different qualities. He would often take sanctuary with an old friend when hard pressed with work and in need of a change of air and scene, taking with him his secretary and chauffeur so as to carry on uninterruptedly his duties without giving his kind host undue trouble.

Lady Battersea was one of those, whose house at Overstrand was always open to B. P., and to me after our marriage. I used to look forward to these visits and listened with delight to her amusing reminiscences of Victorian and Edwardian days, drawn out with great acumen by B. P. A part of her great charm was her 'bird wittedness' (as he called it). Her conversation flitted from subject to subject like a bird hopping from one twig to another; such was the agility of her mind even at her great age. B. P. felt her death very keenly. He often made the remark that one of the sad things about getting old was the losing of old friends. (He had mourned the death of Rivers for fifteen years.) Other friends with whom he often stayed were the Orfords. He baptized, confirmed, and married their only surviving child (the Lady Anne Palmer). Lord Orford's caustic humour greatly amused and stimulated B. P., and he shared with them their intimate joys and griefs.

Lady Quilter, mother of Roger Quilter, was another of B. P.'s early friends, and he often stayed at Bawdsey, and worked from there when the diocese of St. Edmundsbury and Ipswich was still a part of the Norwich diocese. He had some entertaining anecdotes about this very remarkable and able woman, who ruled her large family with great firmness and wisdom long after it had grown up. Lord and Lady Charnwood and their family were others; and latterly, Dame Violet Wills, so well known for her generosity in building churches, and such a good and gentle soul, has been a great friend and ally. There are many others. Of all, I think the most faithful has been the Archdeacon of Norfolk. He and his family have, by their devotion and loving-kindness, shown what true friendship can be; and, through all the vicissitudes and difficulties of administration, and latterly, of retirement, have quietly worked for and with him, and always been at hand with sympathy and understanding.

One of the drawbacks to a busy life is that there is no leisure for getting to know people, so that friendships are, in some cases, limited to the people with whom you are thrown, and it is easy to lose the power to make friends outside this circle. B. P. never lost that power, but he would soon tire of a conversation and excuse himself on the plea of work, disappear into his study, where I would later find him with his legs up, reading *The Times*. There was one worthy baronet (now in a better world) who sometimes put up at the Palace, and whose anecdotes became exhausting rather quickly, who was invariably given a suite of rooms: he protested that he did not like to be treated with 'so much ceremony' (pronouncing it 'Sho much Sheremony')—nevertheless, he continued to have his own sitting-room.

Life at Norwich was very exacting: but B. P. loved work; it was to him the elixir of life; his faith in God was its foundation. He had, to a remarkable degree, the power of concentration and deliberate decision. This, he said, depended upon his getting nine hours' sleep every night. He kept regular hours in so far as such a variety of engagements allowed. His times for prayer (three a day) were never neglected for other work. Important people might be kept waiting for an appointment: "Put him in the antechamber," he would say to the footman, and then in an undertone: "I have an appointment with God." These celestial appointments sometimes caused domestic disturbances, though probably on the whole they prevented many more; and to his unswerving rule of prayer may be attributed his calmness of spirit, his coolness of judgment, his ready sympathy, patience, and great simplicity of faith. He viewed men in the eyes of God, yet withal was very human, enjoying as much as any, a tale of their weaknesses.

His interviews with the clergy took place mostly walking up and down the wide garden paths, whatever the weather, so combining air and exercise with work. Many are the times I have seen his bent form disappearing in the distance, with that rapid swallow-like action, so characteristic and familiar, in a north-easterly gale, a shivering cleric following closely; faint yet pursuing. After one of these interviews he would hurry upstairs to the study and dictate his impressions to his secretary in vividly descriptive language; and then go on to the next interview, and so on.

Other mornings would be taken up with committee meetings, or entirely with correspondence, speech, or sermon writing, and the afternoons with visits to distant parts of the diocese. He made a golden rule of never making any engagements for the day after a visit to London on committee work, so as to catch up any arrears in correspondence. When he was away for more than a day his letters were sent on to him by passenger train. (This was always made easy by the courtesy of the railway officials, and so letters were almost invariably answered by return of post.) One of the footmen was once heard to say: " 'is Lordship is a great man, so 'ee is, but 'ee 'as 'is peculiarities."

Family prayers were a part of the daily routine and took place in the evening, when most of the day's work was done. It was difficult to find a time which suited the whole household. The servants would process in order of rank; the maids in black with white aprons and caps. As the chapel was very cold in winter, and down a draughty stone passage, prayers were 'laid' (as the footmen called it) in one or other of the sitting-rooms. We always had abbreviated evensong, read in B. P.'s inimitable way. The telephone was apt to intervene, giving the servant nearest the door a means of stealthy escape.

The Chapel will, for many people, have undying memories. It was the place in which all our holidays began and ended; with the car at the door, B. P. and I would go there and he would, in the stillness, pray the 'going in and coming out' collect, and the same on our return. In the Chapel there was held, twice or three times a year, a Confirmation for any, young or old, who had been left out in their parish or district. Sometimes boys home on holiday or on leave from the Services, elderly married couples, or the newly married, cripples, or invalids would join together in the intimate little service. B. P. would talk to them seated in a large chair on the chancel steps! (looking more like a Roman Emperor than a prelate) in great simplicity, of the deep things of God. Then he would lay his hands on their heads as they knelt before him, two at a time, praying that beautiful prayer:

Defend, O Lord, this Thy child with Thy heavenly Grace, that he (that she) may continue Thine for ever, and daily increase in Thy Holy Spirit more and more, until he come unto Thy everlasting kingdom.

More vividly do I recall the services of the Clergy Wives' Fellowship, and the Norwich Diocesan Youth Fellowship (of which B. P. has written in this book). The 'specially favourite hymns' (played so well by the Rev. Gordon Paget, who knew how to avoid the organ's many pitfalls), the look of devotion and self-dedication on the faces of the eager young; the hush; and then the quiet, musical voice, telling in perfect diction of the eternal truths; finally, the benediction. These memories will abide.

The garden was a lovely setting for the Cathedral and Palace, with its green lawns and magnificent plane trees; its wide paths and borders flanked by yew hedges centuries old; its ruin of the banqueting hall its great gate under the archway, the steps down which a drunken coachman is reputed to have driven his carriage and pair. The high walls which encircled it and from which B. P. laughingly said the rioters would one day hang him. It was of immense value, this garden on the days of quiet detachment from the things of the world. In it people would walk and talk in twos and threes, or wander alone with their thoughts. It has been observed that 'Quiet Days', though they may be soothing to the tired spirit and refreshing to the mind, are also a splendid medium for the dissemination of news from one end of the diocese to the other. B. P. was fond of telling the story of a large lady who sailed up to him on arrival, rather late, on one of these

ays', and said in a booming voice: "Oh, how d'you do, M'Lord,
erybody is whispering. Have they *all* got colds?"

The advent of our child, Rosalind, was to him a great joy: and as
e grew up, so too there grew a great attachment between them.
e delighted in her childish pleasures, and took a great pride in all
r sayings. When on holiday at our cottage in Suffolk, they would
off together by 'bus to Southwold and walk on the pier. (To
osalind the chief attraction was the penny-in-the-slot machine
presenting a guillotine.) B. P. would watch the old men fishing
r dabs at the end of the pier. They would return like schoolboys
th a bag of *very* soda buns for tea, or sprats bought from a fishing-
at fresh from the sea. B. P. on holiday was a different person to
ok at. He would only be persuaded to discard episcopal garb if he
re outside the diocese, and away for more than three days. Then he
uld appear in a shabby white panama with faded purple ribbon,
d a grey tweed or flannel suit and purple tie; and Rosalind would
nce with delight. Clothes with B. P. were not taken seriously, and
often could be seen hurrying out with his gaiters flapping, and all
t the top button undone, intending to do them up in the train or
eting he was attending. He regarded dress as a covering to the
dy, just as the body might be a covering to the mind and spirit:
t as an expression of personality.

In speaking, as he so often did, of the unseen world, he acquired
timelessness of outlook. I remember when the 1928 Prayer Book
is passed in the House of Lords, and I was condoling with him, he
id: "We are not defeated, we may be working for fifty years ahead."
ue statesmanship does not depend upon manœuvring round the
xt corner as it appears, but rather on getting a bird's-eye view of
e whole situation and keeping the ultimate goal always in sight.
P. possessed that quality in some measure, and, despite his extreme
ution, having once decided that a certain course of action was right,
thing would deflect him from it. This led him to espouse seemingly
t causes; deliberately to lose the friendship of 'time-servers' (some-
nes influential ones), and the support of those he liked and respected.
hen, during the Prayer Book debate, he was referred to as the lonely
arrow twittering on the house-top of the Church, he refused to make
e obvious rejoinder, that the lonely sparrow on the house-top can
e better what is going on in the world around than those sitting in
e house, saying that it might rankle, and adding: "I have never
ed a phrase that I thought would." (Nevertheless, his sparrow-like
sition was soon vindicated publicly by the two rejections of the
vised Prayer Book in the House of Commons.)

His favourite and almost sole literature were the Bible and the

Book of Common Prayer. He read morning and evening prayer ever
day, and the Litany on Sundays. This, he said, embodies all th
yearnings of the human heart in every age for forgiveness and rest
tution, and is never out of date. During Lent he gave up chocolat
(for which he had a great liking) and sugar in coffee, and would dail
read a passage from Farrar's *Life of Christ*, entering deeply into it
rather emotional phases. He would spend the morning of Goo
Friday quite alone in prayer and meditation. He prayed for some o
the clergy of the diocese every day by name, going systematicall
through the diocesan calendar, which was kept by his bedside. H
also prayed in this way for the parishes and churchwardens, whic
may have been the secret of his wonderful memory for the clerg
and their families, and parishes.

Had B. P. lived to finish these recollections and reflections, I fe
sure that he would have included a chapter on 'Norwich,' Holidays, an
Home-life. I have attempted, very feebly, to fill in some of the gap
and to depict, for those who did not know him, his setting. He had
great love of home, and the simplicity of village life appealed to hi
immensely. He had many friends among our near neighbours a
Wenhaston. He loved to wander along the lanes or over the heat
(usually praying, with his eyes on the ground) and then pausing
look up at the beauty of the scenery; to watch the flight of a bir
or to listen for the drumming of the snipe, with a hand to his ea
(He lamented that he had never heard a bat squeak, and could n
longer hear the song of the lark.) And there, below his cottage hom
in the quiet churchyard where he had so often walked and praye
with the marshes and the willows near by, and the wide Suffolk ski
overhead, is laid to rest all that could die of a great and gentle spiri

> Twilight and evening bell,
> And after that the dark!
> And may there be no sadness of farewell
> When I embark;
> For tho' from out our bourne of Time and Place
> The flood may bear me far,
> I hope to see my Pilot face to face
> When I have crossed the bar.

INDEX

BINGER, LORD, 12
Abbots of St. Benet, 77
Addenbrooke's Hospital, 19
Addington Palace, 47
After-dinner Speeches, 144
Airy, Sir George (Astronomer Royal), 13
ALFRED, 133
Amos, the Book of, 106
Anglo-Catholic Clergy, 123, 124, 155
Anonymous letters, 148, 149
Antigone (Sophocles), 52
Archdeacon, Induction by the, 32
—— of Norfolk, 168
Assyrians, Church of the, 47
Atkin, Lord, 143
Auckland Castle, 25, 28
Augustus, Emperor, 71
Aylesbury, Marquess of, 21
—— Marie, Marchioness of, 21

BARONS of the Exchequer, 14
Battersea, Lady, 168
Bawdsey, 168
Bedmakers, College, 18
Beeching, Dr., Dean of Norwich, 80, 81
Bell, G. C., Headmaster of Marlborough, 22
Benefices, Bill relating to, 43
—— Patronage of, 78
Benson, Archbishop of Canterbury, 20, 25, 43–48, 109, 142
—— Arthur C., 44, 98, 99
—— Fred, 44
Bernard, Canon, 28
Bernard of Cluny, 32
Bible, the, 104–115; in the Coronation Service, 84–86; a Spiritual Library, 122, 171
Birkbeck, Mr. J., High Sheriff of Norwich, 85
Birkenhead, Lord, 142, 143
Bishop's Office, A, 77–80; expenses attached to, 78
—— Palace, Norwich, 166–169; the Chapel, 170
Bradley, Dean, 21
Brentford, Lord ('Jix'), 153

Broadcast by the King, 166
Brotherhood, 163–165
Buckmaster, Lord, 143
Burge, Bishop, 134
Burial Service, the, 104
Burnham Thorpe, 158
Butler, Dr., Master of Trinity College, Cambridge, 75

CALDECOTE, Lord, 153
Cambridge, 16, 112
—— H.R.H. the Duke of, 105
Candidates for Confirmation, 63, 64
—— Ordination, 29, 32, 78
Canterbury Cathedral, 48
Carisbrooke, Lord, 66
Carlisle Cathedral, 48
Carnock, Lord, 58
Carr, C. Lisle, Bishop of Hereford, 81
Carson, Lord, 153
Catullus, 7
Cavell, Edith, 157, 158
—— Mrs., 157
Cecil, Lord William, Bishop of Exeter, 153
Charnwood, Lord and Lady, 168
Charterhouse, 16, 17
Chichester, Bishop of, 139
Christmas at Sandringham, 90
Church and people, 120–124
—— of England, the, 30, 31, 103, 133–136
—— Society, the, 19
Clergy, the, 94, 123, 124, 155
—— Wives' Fellowship, 93, 170
Codex Sinaiticus, 112, 114, 115
Communion of Saints, the, 103
Confirmation, 63, 64, 77, 78, 170
Connaught, H.R.H. The Duke of, 37–39
Coronation of George V and Queen Mary, 83
—— George VI and Queen Elizabeth, 83–86
—— Service, 132
Convocation, 120
Corunna, 13
Cotton, Bishop, 22

Cowper, 74
Cranage, Dr., Dean of Norwich, 82, 83
Crewe, Lord, 142
Crossing the Bar (Tennyson), 56, 172
Cuddesdon, 75
Curzon, Lord, 143
Cushenden, Lord, 153

DAVIDSON, Archbishop of Canterbury, 44, 45, 75, 96, 120, 129, 130, 137, 142, 151, 155
D'Arcy of Armagh, Archbishop, 131
Darwin, 13, 14
Dean of Arches, the, 160
Deans of Norwich, 80–83
De Contemptu Mundi, 32
Derby, Lord, 38
Devizes, 23
Dibdin, Sir Lewis, 130
Dilapidations Measure (1923), 127
Disendowment, 135
Disestablishment, 130–136
Disraeli, 144
Dominions, the, 132
Donaldson, Bishop of Salisbury, 19

Eastern Daily Press, 95
Education Bill, the New, 56, 61
EDWARD VII, 33–37, 59, 70, 71; the Peacemaker, 72, 81–84; at Sandringham, 87, 88
EDWARD VIII, 55, 73, 84
Enabling Act, the, 120
Erastianism, 131

FAITH, 115–119
Family Prayers, 169
Fanshawe, Sir Arthur, Admiral of the Fleet, 55
Free Churches, the, 94, 125, 130, 135
Frere, Bishop of Truro, 19
Frogmore, 160

GEORGE III, 11, 69
GEORGE V, 36, 72, 73; Coronation of, 83, 88; at Sandringham, 90
GEORGE VI, Coronation of, 83–86; 104, 109
Gladstone, Mr., 47

Gore, Dr., Bishop of Birmingham, 8 142
Goldsmith, Oliver, 159
Goulburn, Dean, 83
Great Eastern Hotel, 94
Greece, a Lecture on, 49
Greeks, 53
Greenwich, 12

HAIG-BROWN, Dr., 17
Haldane, Lord, 52, 143
Hamilton, Lord Claud, 94
Hannah, Mr., 85
Hanworth, Lord, Master of the Roll 15, 20, 167
Hastings, Lord, 143, 144
Hawkins, Judge, 23
Heart of Midlothian, The (Scott), 11
Hebrew, 18, 28
Henry, Duke of Wellington, 24
HENRY VIII, 40, 77
Herbert, Rev. Henry, 13
History of England, The (Trevelyan 134
Holman Hunt, 106
Holy Communion (Bertram Pollock), 3
Holy Matrimony, 152
Home-life, Clerical, 158
Horace, 5, 15, 17, 145
Hort, Professor, 25
Horton Smith, 21
'Hotel Divorces', 150
House of Commons, 12
—— of Lords, 77, 137–140

Ignorance of Man, The (Butler), 30
Illustrated London News, 14, 47
Ipswich, 168
Iron Duke, the, 4, 44, 68

JERICHO, Capture of, 108
Jerusalem Chamber, Westminste Abbey, 111
Johnson, Guy, 153
Juvenal, 80

KING, Elizabeth ('Lizzy'), 14, 167
Kingship, the Art of, 72
Kipling, Rudyard, 146
Knox, Bishop, 153

LANG, Archbishop Lord, 142
Lambeth Palace, 44, 47
Leicester, Lord, 32
Lecky, 124
Lee, Prince, Bishop of Manchester, 46
Legge, Mrs., 57
Letters and Letter-writing, 96
LEOPOLD II, King of the Belgians, 91
Life of Bishop Blomfield, 40, 64
Life of Christ (Farrar), 22, 172
Lightfoot, Bishop, 68
Lincoln, Bishop of, 46
Lincolnshire, Lord, 153
Lind, Jenny, 14
Little Arthur's History of England, 13
Lloyd George, Mr., 144
L.N.E.R., 94
Lord Mayor, the, 14
—— —— of Norwich, the, 45
Lucretius, 18
Ludham, 77

MAGEE, Bishop, 142
Malvern, 5, 48
Marlborough, 5, 20–24, 92
Marlborough House, 24
Marriage, 150–153
Memorials in Churches, 159
Memorial effigies of Prince Albert and Queen Victoria, 160
Minns, Professor, 115
Missionaries, 64
Moule, Bishop, 118
Munro, H. A. J., 18
Murray, John, 13, 31

NAVY, Examinations for the, 54
Nelson, 158
New Prayer Book, 153
Norris, Dr. Foxley, Dean of Westminster, 85
Norfolk, Duke of, Earl Marshal, 84
—— Chief Constable of, 94
Norwich, 24, 25, 28, 77, 92
—— Cathedral, 82
—— Chief Constable of, 94
—— Diocese of, 75, 76
—— Hospital, 94
—— Lord Mayor of, 45
Norwood Report, the, 56

ORFORD, Lord, 168
Origin of Species (Darwin), 13, 14
Overstrand, 165
Oxford Movement, the, 123, 131
—— University Press, 84

PAGE, T. E., 17
Paget, Francis, Bishop of Oxford, 75
—— Sir George, 19
—— Rev. Gordon, 170
—— Miss, 19
Palmer, Lady Anne, 168
Parentage, Bishop Pollock's, 3
Parish, the, 122
Parsonage and People, 158
Peache, Miss, 16
Persius, 7
Pierce, Ruth, 23
Police, the, 94
Pollock, Bertram, K.C.V.O., D.D., late Bishop of Norwich, 3–8; autobiography, 3–165; tribute by Mrs Pollock, 166–172
—— Mrs. Bertram (née Joan Ryder), 30, 167–172
—— Ernest, Lord Hanworth, 15, 20, 167
—— Sir Frederick, 11, 12
—— Haddie, 14
—— Rivers, M.D., 19, 167
—— Rosalind, 171
Ponsonby, Lord, 71
Pope, the, 124
Prayer, 99–103
Prayer Book of 1928, 153–157
Press, the, 94, 95, 155, 156
Prime Minister, the, 166
Prince Arthur, 68
—— Christian, 35
—— Consort, the, 4, 33, 46
—— of Wales, 24, 33
Princess Beatrice, 66, 67
Probyn, Sir Dighton, 34, 88
Public School System, Our, 54
—— —— Punishment, 52, 53
—— —— Religious Training, 61–65

QUEEN ALEXANDRA, 35, 39, 87, 88
—— ELIZABETH, 74; Coronation of, 83–86
—— MARY, 73, 83, 87–92

QUEEN VICTORIA, 37, 46, 59, 66–72, 79, 109, 160
Queen's Remembrancer, 11
Quickswood, Lord, 156
Quilter, Lady, 168
—— Roger, 168

REVISED VERSION, the, 109–114
Roberts, Field-Marshal Lord, 145
Roman Church, the, 136
—— Clergy, the, 124
Rosebery, Lord, 144
Rose Crescent, Cambridge, 18
—— Day, Queen Alexandra's, 88
Royal Family, the, 33, 36
Ryder, Rev. Algernon Dudley, 30
—— Joan, 30

SAINT AUGUSTINE, 63
Saint Paul's, 75
Salisbury, 28
—— Professor, 138
Sandringham, 87, 88
Savernake Forest, 20
Scapegoat in the Wilderness (painting), 51
School reports, 42, 43
Scotland, the Church of, 134
Senate House, Cambridge, the, 19
Sergeant arrests the Bishop, a, 149
Simmons, Sir Lintorn, 67
Simon, Lord, 142
Snell, Lord, 3
Southwold, 171
Statesmanship, true, 171
Stonehenge, 23, 99
Stubbs, Bishop, 44
Sumner, Lord, 143
Swete, Dr., 20

TAIT, Archbishop, 141
Talbot, Sir P., 24

Temple, Archbishop, 133
Tennyson, 7
Thackeray, 17
The Times, 138, 155, 156
Thompson, O.M., Sir J. J., 19
Thucydides, 16
Trevelyan, O.M., George, Master of Trinity, 134
Trinity College, Cambridge, 18
Tyndale, 109

VATICAN LIBRARY, 114
Verrall, A. W., 18
Virgil, 7, 146

WADDELL, Miss Helen, 52
Wakefield, Dr. Russell, 80
Westcott, Bishop of Durham, 25–28, 45, 46, 111, 154
Wellington, Duke of, 44, 68
—— College, 4, 38–44, 47
—— —— laying of foundation stone, 66–68
—— —— visit of Queen Victoria, 66
—— —— visit of Edward VII, 34
Whittington, Bishop, 127
Wickham, Dr., 5
Willet, Mr., 60
Wilson, Sir Henry, 145
Wimbledon, Vicar of, 16
Windsor Castle, 70
Wokingham, 46
Wordsworth, John, Bishop of Salisbury, 25
—— Bishop of Lincoln, 25
World to come, the, 119

YORK, Archbishop of, 142
—— Assizes, 11
Young, G. M., 138

Zoo, the, 15